IBM® PC DOS and Microsoft® Windows™ User's Guide

S0-BAU-737

que
COLLEGE

Acknowledgments

Thanks to the IBM PC DOS team in Boca for its technical review of this book.

Author

Suzanne Weixel

Publisher

David P. Ewing

Publishing Manager

Chris Katsaropoulos

Managing Editor

Sheila B. Cunningham

Senior Editor

Jeannine Freudenberger

Production Editor

Fran Blauw

Editor

Beth Hux

Technical Editors

Rolf A. Crozier
Doug White

Acquisitions Coordinator

Elizabeth D. Brown

Book Designer

Paula Carroll

Production Team

Steve Adams
Chad Dressler
Karen L. Gregor
Bob LaRoche
G. Alan Palmore
Linda Quigley
Mike Thomas

Indexers

Michael Hughes
Craig Small

Composed in *Stone Serif* and *Courier* by Que Corporation.

Contents at a Glance

Table of Contents

9 Controlling the Printer   193

11 Using Stacker Compression   245

Introduction

By itself, a computer is just a box and a screen. Ultimately, you are faced with the challenge of bringing it to life. This means mastering the computer's operating system, which is PC DOS.

No matter what you may have heard, PC DOS isn't a hostile environment that only people with advanced degrees in computer engineering can master. PC DOS is a tool that people at all levels use to manage the information that computers store in files.

PC DOS does depend on the keyboard, however, and it does rely on commands that must be typed correctly. Everyone who uses PC DOS is familiar with the message `Bad command or file name` that appears when you mistype a command or file name.

With Windows, you can access the power of PC DOS without committing a single command to memory. You can use a mouse to point and click your way among pictures and plain English words to accomplish disk- and file-management tasks—without touching a keyboard. When used together, IBM PC DOS and Windows make controlling your computer a pleasure, not a chore.

What Does This Book Contain?

Each chapter in the *IBM PC DOS and Microsoft Windows User's Guide* is built around a set of related tasks. The chapters are organized so that you can use the information they present to accomplish the tasks. In addition, the chapters are grouped into parts. You don't have to read the book sequentially to learn to use IBM PC DOS and Windows. Feel free to jump around from chapter to chapter and section to section to find the information you want.

From beginning to end, the chapters move from the basics—from understanding your computer system, to using common PC DOS and Windows commands; and then into more advanced tasks, such as customizing your desktop, configuring your computer, safeguarding your system and data, and compressing your data.

Part I: PC Basics

In Chapter 1, "Understanding System Basics," you are introduced to the hardware and software components of your computer.

In Chapter 2, "Making PC DOS Work," you learn how to use PC DOS to manage your files and disks, and how to get help when you need it.

In Chapter 3, "Working with the Windows Desktop," you learn how to start and exit Windows, and how to recognize the different parts of the Windows desktop.

In Chapter 4, "Making Windows Work," you learn how to manage the Windows desktop and how to use the Program Manager to organize your programs.

In Chapter 5, "Using File Manager," you learn to use the Windows File Manager to manage your files and disks.

Part II: Beyond the Basics

In Chapter 6, "Customizing Your Desktop," you learn to set up the Windows desktop to suit your own particular needs.

In Chapter 7, "Working with the Text Editor," you learn to edit ASCII files with the E Editor.

In Chapter 8, "Configuring Your Personal Computer," you explore the different ways you can use the AUTOEXEC.BAT and CONFIG.SYS files to set up your computing environment and how to optimize your computer's memory usage.

In Chapter 9, "Controlling the Printer," you learn how to set up your printer for use in Windows and how to make the most of available fonts and printer drivers.

In Chapter 10, "Using PC DOS 7.0 Tools," you learn about using PC DOS to safeguard your hardware and software. The chapter covers the PC DOS utility tools: AntiVirus, Backup, Undelete, and Defrag. In addition, you learn about the MSCDEX command, PenDOS, and PCMCIA-based features (for users who have a computer equipped with a CD-ROM drive, a PCMCIA memory card, or a pen-based application). You also learn about the REXX programming language, the File Update program that helps keep files synchronized and up-to-date, and how to use Interlnk to connect two PCs.

Finally, in Chapter 11, "Using Stacker Compression," you learn what a data-compression program does, why users need one, and how to use the Stacker compression program that comes with PC DOS 7.0.

Who Should Use This Book?

The *IBM PC DOS and Microsoft Windows User's Guide* is a useful book for anyone who wants to get the most from a personal computer that is running both IBM PC DOS and Windows. Although the book is useful for everyone, it is designed especially for new computer users, casual users, or users who don't need to or want to learn everything about PC DOS and Windows. The book presents enough basic information to get you started if you are a first-time user and then builds on your growing understanding by introducing more advanced topics.

Where to Find More Help

After you master the features in this book, you may want to learn more about the advanced capabilities of PC DOS and Windows. If so, you can turn to Que's *Using Windows 3.11*, Special Edition, which can be purchased from retail stores.

Both PC DOS and Windows provide extensive on-line help to answer many of your questions. To learn about getting help with using PC DOS commands, see Chapter 2, "Making PC DOS Work." To learn about getting help with using Windows, see Chapter 4, "Making Windows Work."

Conventions Used in This Book

This book has certain conventions to help you use and understand the information that is presented:

- Keys that you press and text that you type appear in **boldface** type. The text you type is UPPERCASE, although you usually can type either uppercase or lowercase.

- Key combinations, such as **Ctrl+Enter**, indicate that you should press and hold down the first key as you press the second key.

- Important words or phrases appear in *italics* the first time they are discussed.

- Screen displays and messages appear in a `special typeface`.

- Menu commands appear as "Choose **F**ile, **R**un." To use these commands, you use the mouse to click the File menu and then click the Run option on that menu. Alternatively, you can press **Alt+F** and then press **R**.

- **Notes** provide information that might help you avoid problems or accomplish some task in a more efficient manner.

- **Keywords** in the margins briefly define new terms that you encounter as you read this book.

- **If you have problems...** paragraphs provide troubleshooting information to help you escape from problem situations.

Part I
PC Basics

Chapter 1

Understanding System Basics

"Using a computer is easy." You've heard that statement before. It's the kind of glib remark that might make you wish for an adding machine and ballpoint pen instead of a computer.

Personal computers are logical. They function according to very strict, straightforward rules and guidelines. All you have to do is learn the rules, and you can take charge of the computer on your desk. Luckily, the application programs written for computers are continually becoming easier to use; the combination of PC DOS and Windows (two pieces of software that are explained in the following section) makes learning the rules easier than ever.

With PC DOS and Windows, you can access all the power of your computer. Before you put your computer to work, however, you need to understand its components, and you need to know how those components work together. This chapter describes the relationship between personal computer hardware and the operating system.

Understanding Your Computer System

Hardware
The physical parts of the computer that you can see and touch.

All personal computers consist of the same basic *hardware* components:

- *System Unit*. The system unit is the box that holds all the electrical components of your computer, as well as some peripheral devices, such as disk drives and modems.

- *Keyboard*. You use the keyboard to communicate with the computer by typing entries and issuing commands. Computer keyboards are similar to typewriter keyboards; they have all the traditional letter and punctuation keys. Computer keyboards also have special keys such as Alt, Ctrl, Esc, Enter, and the arrow keys.

■ *Display*. The display shows on-screen what you type at the keyboard.

■ *Diskette drive*. The diskette drive (also called the floppy disk drive) is the door into your computer. The computer reads information from and writes information to the diskettes you insert into the drive.

Hard disk

A fixed magnetic device used to store computer files.

■ *Hard disk drive*. The hard disk drive stores the application programs and data files with which you work.

■ *Mouse*. The mouse is a pointing device that enables you to move the mouse pointer on-screen, select objects, and issue commands.

■ *Printer*. The printer makes a paper copy of the data that you create on the computer. To print anything, you need to attach and install a printer.

All computers have the same basic hardware components.

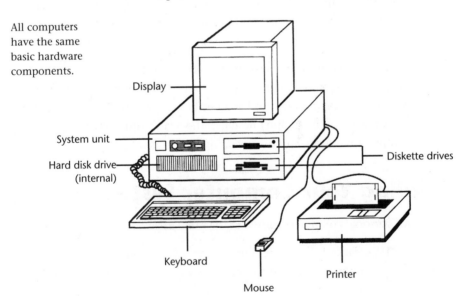

Display

System unit

Hard disk drive
(internal)

Diskette drives

Keyboard

Mouse

Printer

As long as your computer has these main components, the shape and size of your computer does not matter. For example, you can find equally powerful machines in the traditional desktop and tower systems, in floor models, in portable laptop models, or in notebook computers.

Software
Program and data files created, stored, and run by your computer. These terms—applications, software, and programs—often are used interchangeably.

By itself, a computer is just an appliance made of plastic and metal, not so different from a toaster oven. To bring the computer to life, you need *software*.

Software programs designed for use on personal computers fall into two basic types:

■ *System software*. Controls the way the different pieces of hardware operate and the way the computer responds to commands. PC DOS and Windows are both examples of system software.

■ *Application software*. Enables you to perform specific tasks, such as word processing, desktop publishing, or spreadsheet tasks. Microsoft Word and Lotus 1-2-3 are examples of application software.

Understanding PC DOS

Disk operating system
A system software program that controls the way a computer processes information.

PC DOS (to many computer users, just DOS) is a tool you use to manage the information your computer stores in disk files. DOS stands for *disk operating system*. PC DOS is a collection of programs and standard routines that enables you to communicate with your computer and enables your computer to communicate with hardware devices.

You cannot accomplish anything on your computer without PC DOS. The computer and application programs alone are useless. With PC DOS, however, you can issue commands, start application programs, and manage information.

Interface
A point of communication between you and your computer or between different components of the computer.

With PC DOS, you can interact with your computer through either of two *interfaces*:

■ *PC DOS command prompt*. The line in which you can type commands by using precise command syntax. For more information, see the section "Typing PC DOS Commands," later in this chapter.

The PC DOS command prompt, which looks like the following, indicates that PC DOS is waiting for you to enter commands:

c:\>

After the PC DOS command prompt, you use the keyboard to type the commands.

■ *PC DOS Shell*. A window displaying menus, dialog boxes, and icons that you can use to enter commands. For more information, see the section "Using the PC DOS Shell," later in this chapter.

In the PC DOS Shell, you communicate with PC DOS by using the mouse, menu commands, and icons.

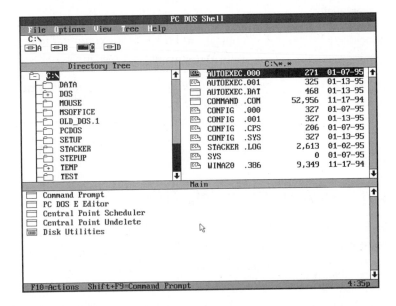

IBM updates PC DOS periodically by adding new commands and making other commands work better. Each time a new version is released, it gets a new number. If the changes are minor, only the number to the right of the decimal point changes. If the changes are significant, the number to the left of the decimal point changes. The most current version is PC DOS 7.0.

Understanding Windows

Graphical user interface

A visual interface that combines graphics, menus, and commands that you use to communicate with your computer.

Microsoft Windows is a *graphical user interface* (GUI), which makes it even easier for you to use PC DOS to communicate with your computer. Windows displays icons, menus, and dialog boxes so that you can see exactly what you are doing and what tools you are using at all times. These displayed elements follow:

- *Icon.* A small picture used to represent a system component or command on-screen.

- *Menu.* A list of commands.

- *Dialog box.* A window in which you can enter information that PC DOS or another application program needs in order to continue processing a command (not shown in the following figure).

Windows is a graphical user interface that enables you to communicate with your computer through icons, menus, and dialog boxes.

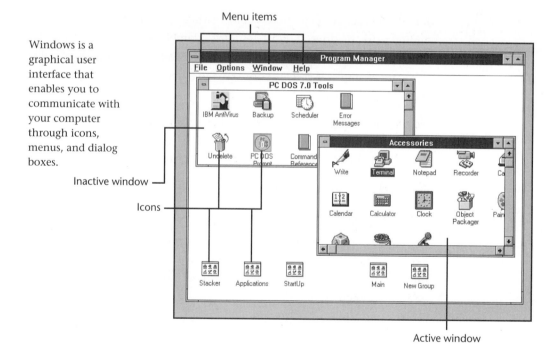

The design of Windows is based on the concept that your computer should be like your desktop. With Windows, you can keep many different files and projects available at the same time and switch among them by reaching for the one you need—just as if it were on your desk.

For more information about using Windows, see Chapter 3, "Working with the Windows Desktop," and Chapter 4, "Making Windows Work."

Understanding Disks and Disk Drives

Disk drive
A hardware device that reads from and writes data to magnetic storage disks.

Diskette
A removable magnetic device used to store computer files.

Your computer stores information that is not currently in use on a magnetic storage disk in a *disk drive*. Disk drives usually are installed inside the system unit, although some are attached externally with cables.

There are two basic types of disk drives: *diskette* (or floppy) and hard. Computers can contain more than one disk drive and more than one disk drive type. Most computers come with at least one hard disk drive and one diskette drive, but different drive combinations are common. Your computer can have two diskette drives in addition to one hard drive, for example. If you are connected to a network, your computer may not have a hard disk drive at all.

No matter how many disk drives you have, they follow the same naming scheme: the first diskette drive is named drive A, the second is named drive B. The first hard disk is named drive C, and so on.

Diskettes

Diskettes come in two sizes: 5 1/4-inch and 3 1/2-inch.

Each drive uses only one size or the other. If you have a 5 1/4-inch drive, you must use 5 1/4-inch diskettes. If you have a 3 1/2-inch drive, you must use 3 1/2-inch diskettes. Your computer can have both a 5 1/4-inch and a 3 1/2-inch drive.

A 5 1/4-inch
diskette fits in a
5 1/4-inch drive.

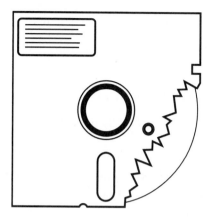

A 3 1/2-inch
diskette fits in a
3 1/2-inch drive.

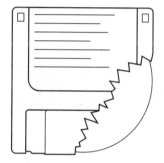

Capacity
The measure of the
amount of data that
can be stored on a
disk.

Diskettes also come in different *capacities*, which are measured in kilo-bytes (abbreviated *K*) or in megabytes (abbreviated *M*, *MB*, or *meg*). One byte equals approximately one typed character. One kilobyte equals approximately one thousand bytes (1,024 to be exact), and one megabyte equals approximately one million bytes.

The 5 1/4-inch diskettes come in two capacities:

- 360K, double-density diskettes can store about 360,000 characters of information.

- 1.2M, high-density diskettes can store 1.2 million bytes.

The 3 1/2-inch diskettes come in three capacities:

- 720K, double-density diskettes can store about 720,000 characters of information.

- 1.44M, high-density diskettes can store 1.44 million bytes.

- 2.88M diskettes can store 2.88 million bytes.

Format
To prepare a diskette for use by PC DOS.

To prepare a diskette for use, you must *format* it. (Some companies sell preformatted diskettes, however.) Keep in mind that you must format a diskette to the correct capacity. That is, you cannot buy a 360K diskette and then format it as a 1.2M diskette.

Hard Disks

Hard disks can store more information than diskettes store. Each hard disk drive contains many disks, or platters, all of which are used to store data.

A hard disk drive contains many disks, which are used to store data.

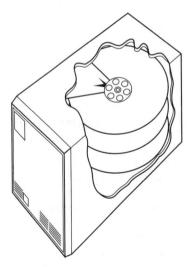

Hard disk capacities are measured in megabytes and come in various sizes: 20M, 30M, 40M, 60M, 80M, 100M, and up.

Average access time
The speed with which a disk drive can find data stored on a disk.

Hard disks are more durable than diskettes. Hard disks are fixed inside the disk drive, which usually is encased inside the system unit. For this reason, they are not as susceptible to dirt and damage as diskettes.

Hard disk drives access information on a disk faster than diskette drives. Most hard drives have *average access times* of between 15 and 20 milliseconds.

Understanding Disk Organization

Think about how you store items in your office. You may have a filing cabinet in which you keep folders containing information that pertains to different projects, clients, patients, or some other group—maybe logical, maybe not. Within each folder, you have articles, letters, diagrams, or reports—anything you want to save.

Directory
On a disk, a group of files and other directories that PC DOS uses to locate data.

PC DOS offers you a similar storage method for keeping track of data. You use a disk the same way you use a filing cabinet. On each disk, you create *directories* that provide the same function as a file folder in a filing cabinet. Within the directories, you store files—the same items you would store in a file folder—memos, articles, diagrams, and so on.

Understanding Directory Hierarchy

Directory tree
A diagram showing the organization of directories and files on a disk.

On a disk, the organization of directories is hierarchical, which means that layers of directories grow out of one main directory. Because directories on a disk look like the connected branches of a tree, a diagram of the directories is called a *directory tree*. The main directory, out of which all the other directories grow, is called the *root directory*.

In the PC DOS directory structure, the root directory is the top directory.

Root Directory
The main directory on a disk, out of which all other directories grow.

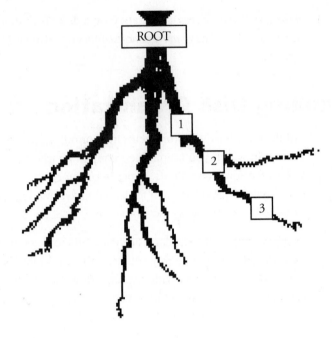

The numbered boxes represent directories on branches of the tree-structured hierarchy.

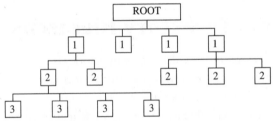

In PC DOS, the root directory is designated by a single backslash (\). To identify a directory other than the root, the backslash is followed by the other directory's name, as in C:\DOS\DATA.

Path
The list of directories, starting with the root, that leads to a specific file.

Directories can contain other directories or files. To perform any action or command on a file, you must tell PC DOS exactly where on the directory tree the file is located. To do so, you specify the *path* from the disk drive, referred to as drive A, B, C, and so on. The path specifies the route PC DOS travels to find a file—from the root directory, possibly through several other directories, to the directory that contains the file, and all the way to the file itself.

Subdirectory
Sometimes directories other than the root are called subdirectories. However, the terms are interchangeable.

When you specify a path, you separate each pair of directory names by a backslash (\). For example, the path

C:\WORD\REPORTS

gives PC DOS these directions: start at drive C, go from the root directory (\) to the directory named WORD, and then go to the *subdirectory* named REPORTS.

Understanding Files

File
A collection of data stored as a unit on a disk.

Most of the data you use on your computer is organized into *files*. You create the files using your application programs. Every word processing document is a file, for example. Every spreadsheet is also a file, and so on.

Even though you create the files when you are using the application programs, you use PC DOS to organize and manage the files. You must follow PC DOS rules when you create and name files.

Naming Files and Directories

You name files and directories to help you identify their contents and to help PC DOS to find them on a disk.

Extension
A three-letter suffix added to a file name that describes the file's contents.

An entire file name is made up of two parts: the file name, which can be up to eight characters long; and an optional file name *extension*, which can be three characters long. The file name and extension are separated by a period.

As discussed earlier in this chapter, the backslash symbol is used alone to identify the root directory. To identify a directory other than the root, the backslash symbol is followed by a directory name. Directory names, like file names, can be up to eight characters long. Directory names do not usually include extensions.

You cannot use these characters in a file or directory name:

' / \ [ ] : ; + = , * ? and | (the vertical bar symbol)

REPORT.DOC is a valid file name. REPORT is the file name, and DOC is the extension. The file name should tell you what the report contains; the extension often tells you the type of file. Some application programs assign an extension automatically.

MY NOTES is not a valid file name because a file name cannot contain spaces. If you want to separate words in a file name, you can use the underline character, as in MY_NOTES.

Note: *You should give some thought to file and directory names. Names should clearly identify the contents of the item.*

Within one directory, subdirectories and files must have unique names. However, you can have another subdirectory or file with the same name if it is stored in another directory. You can have a file named MEMO.DOC stored in both the LETTERS subdirectory on drive C, and in the BUDGET subdirectory on drive C, for example. You cannot have two files named MEMO.DOC in the LETTERS subdirectory.

Using Wild Cards

Wild cards
Characters used to represent one or more characters.

When you want to work with a group of files, you can type *wild cards* within file names in commands given at the PC DOS command prompt. There are two wild cards: the asterisk (*) and the question mark (?).

The question mark (?) wild card is used in place of any single character.

The asterisk (*) wild card is used in place of a single character and all the characters that follow it in a file name or extension—until you type another character.

File spec
An abbreviation for file specification. The complete name and path to a file stored on a disk.

You can use wild cards in different combinations to control which files are included in a group. Suppose that you are writing a book that has eight chapters. The file for each chapter is named CHAP, followed by the chapter number, a period, and the file extension DOC. When you want to copy all the files (CHAP1.DOC through CHAP8.DOC), you can use a *file spec* such as:

CHAP?.DOC

This file spec uses the ? wild card and tells PC DOS to include every file name beginning with *CHAP* and followed by any single character and the *DOC* extension. Remember that each ? wild card represents only one character.

Suppose that your book contains 15 chapters and the files are named CHAP1.DOC through CHAP15.DOC. You need to use a different wild card—the asterisk. To copy all the files for this book, you can use a file spec such as

CHAP*.DOC

This file spec tells PC DOS to include every file name beginning with *CHAP*, followed by any number of characters and the *DOC* extension. Remember that the * wild card represents any number of characters.

Special Files

Your computer contains three special files that you should understand:

CONFIG.SYS

AUTOEXEC.BAT

COMMAND.COM

When you start PC DOS, it looks for a file named AUTOEXEC.BAT. This file must be stored in the root directory. PC DOS finds the file and carries out its instructions. This file can include commands that control different settings you want to use every time you start your computer. You might include a PATH command that tells PC DOS where your application programs are located, for example.

Configuration
The way the hardware and software of a computer are set up or organized.

Another special file that PC DOS uses when it starts is CONFIG.SYS, a *configuration* file. Some application programs require special commands. These commands are contained in the CONFIG.SYS file. Settings in the CONFIG.SYS file control the way PC DOS uses files, memory, application programs, and hardware devices.

To process commands, you must have a file named COMMAND.COM. COMMAND.COM is the command processor. It contains the most commonly used PC DOS commands. When you install PC DOS, this file is copied to the hard drive.

When dealing with these special files, keep these rules in mind:

- Don't delete COMMAND.COM, AUTOEXEC.BAT, or CONFIG.SYS.

- Don't try to change the contents of COMMAND.COM.

■ As you add application programs to the computer, the documentation may tell you to make changes to the AUTOEXEC.BAT file or the CONFIG.SYS file, or the application program itself may automatically make these changes. Be careful when making any changes to these files. You should understand each command in the file before changing anything. Also, it is a good idea to keep a copy of the original versions of these files in case something goes wrong with the new files.

Note: *For more information on the CONFIG.SYS and AUTOEXEC.BAT files, see Chapter 8, "Configuring Your Personal Computer."*

Understanding the PC DOS Shell

Since Version 5.0, PC DOS has included its own built-in graphical user interface: the PC DOS Shell. Rather than use the command line to enter commands, you can enter commands through the Shell.

The PC DOS Shell view is a full-screen graphical window. You can issue most PC DOS commands by using a mouse or the keyboard to point to and select pull-down menus and dialog boxes. You do not have to remember the names of commands to use the PC DOS Shell. You just select actions from menus, type answers to questions, and check options in dialog boxes.

The Shell view is the friendliest way to use PC DOS. A directory listing is automatic when you are in the PC DOS Shell, for example. You always see a listing of the subdirectories and files in the current directory.

PC DOS Shell is one of the PC DOS 7 optional tools. You install PC DOS Shell on your computer during PC DOS 7 installation. If you did not install PC DOS Shell during installation, you can go back and install it at any time.

After you install PC DOS Shell, PC DOS 7 configures your system to automatically load the PC DOS Shell whenever you start your computer.

If someone has changed your PC's configuration so that when you start your computer you see the command line instead of the Shell, you still can start the Shell. To start the PC DOS Shell from the PC DOS command prompt, type **DOSSHELL** and press Enter.

Looking at the PC DOS Shell

When you start the PC DOS Shell, you see a full-screen display. This initial screen shows you the list of disk drives in your computer, the files in the root directory, and a list of some of the PC DOS programs available.

The PC DOS Shell can be displayed in different modes and colors. If you have a text-only display, the Shell appears in text mode. If you have a graphics display, the Shell appears in graphics mode.

If you have a graphics display, you can show the PC DOS Shell in graphics mode. In graphics mode, the Shell uses icons to represent disk drives, directories, programs, and text files. Other parts of the display, such as the scroll bars and the mouse pointer, are easier to view in graphics mode. You can preview and change display modes by choosing **D**isplay from the **O**ptions menu.

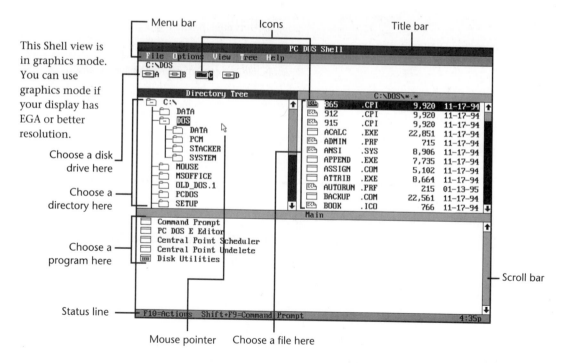

This Shell view is in graphics mode. You can use graphics mode if your display has EGA or better resolution.

No matter which mode you use to display the PC DOS Shell, the same basic parts appear on-screen. Table 1.1 describes the basic parts of the Shell display.

Table 1.1 PC DOS Shell Parts

Part	Description
Title bar	Identifies the name of the current window or dialog box.
Menu bar	Provides a list of pull-down menu options. The menu bar is below the title bar of the main window.
Disk drive area	Lists the disk drives your computer recognizes. The selected drive is highlighted.
Directory tree	Identifies the Directory Tree area. The title is highlighted when the area is selected.
Directory tree area	Shows the directories for the selected drive. The selected directory is highlighted.
Files area title	Identifies the Files area. The title is highlighted when this area is selected.
Files area	Shows the files for the selected directory. The selected file is highlighted.
Program area title	Identifies the program area. The title is highlighted when this area is selected.
Program area	Lists the programs available from the current program group and lists other program groups.
Selection cursor	In text mode, the selection cursor is a small triangular arrow. In graphics mode, it indicates the selected drive, directory, file, or program with a highlighted area or band.
Status line	Shows function key commands, messages, and the current time at the bottom line of the Shell display.
Mouse pointer	Indicates the current position of the mouse on the display.
Scroll bar	Used to view any list of directories, files, or programs that is too long to fit in the display area.

Using the PC DOS Shell

Remember that to start the PC DOS Shell from the PC DOS command prompt, you must follow these steps:

1. Type **DOSSHELL**.

2. Press **Enter**.

From the Shell, you can execute PC DOS commands, run application programs, find files, view the contents of files, and change the way that the Shell display appears. All these actions are performed by selecting menu options. You do not have to remember command names or the format and parameters of the commands. Just browse through the Shell to see the available commands.

Although you can use either the keyboard or the mouse in PC DOS Shell, it is much easier to use a mouse. With a mouse, you can simply click on the command you want to use or the item you want to select. If you have a keyboard, you can use the arrow keys or the Tab key to move around the PC DOS Shell screen, and key combinations to select commands. Many commands can be executed using shortcut keys, as well.

To open the File menu, for example, you can click the word `File` with your mouse, or you can press **Alt+F**. **Alt** is the key that makes the menu bar active, and **F** is the highlighted letter in the **F**ile command name.

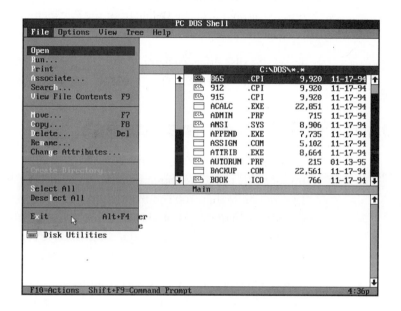

If you decide that you want to enter a command from the standard command line instead of the Shell, you can choose Exit from the File menu (click **F**ile and then click E**x**it, or press **Alt+F** and then press **X**), press **Alt+F4** (the Exit shortcut key combination), or press **F3**.

You can return temporarily to the PC DOS command line without exiting from the Shell by pressing **Shift+F9**. To return to the PC DOS Shell, type **EXIT** at the PC DOS command prompt.

When PC DOS needs you to supply more information to complete a command, it displays a dialog box. You type the answers to the prompts and choose OK, and PC DOS carries out the command.

If an item on the Shell screen is highlighted, that item is selected. When one of the disk drive letters is highlighted, that drive is the selected drive, and the list of directories in the Directory Tree area is for the selected drive. When one of the directories in the displayed list is highlighted, this directory is the selected directory, and the list of files in the Files area is for the selected directory. If there are more files than can fit in the Files area, the scroll bar is highlighted. Click the up or down arrow to display the rest of the file list.

Before you use other Shell commands, you must know which items are selected. The command you select affects the selected items. If a file is selected and you choose **D**elete from the **F**ile menu, for example, the selected file is deleted.

To select a disk drive, click the disk drive icon. To select a directory, click the directory folder icon. To select a file, click the file icon.

Typing PC DOS Commands

To use PC DOS from the PC DOS command prompt, you have to communicate by using the command names that PC DOS understands. PC DOS has more than 100 commands, although you may use only 10 or 12 of them regularly. Most of the command names describe the actions they initiate. COPY, for example, is the command for copying a file, and DIR is the command for displaying a list of the contents of a directory.

You type a command into PC DOS to the right of the PC DOS command prompt. Then you press **Enter** to issue the command. PC DOS processes the command and responds accordingly.

Syntax
The precise format you must use when you type a command.

PC DOS is particular about the way you type a command. If you don't get the *syntax* exactly right, PC DOS cannot process the command. If you do not enter spaces in the correct location, for example, PC DOS does not recognize the command.

If you make a mistake when typing, you can press **Backspace** to delete characters before you press **Enter**. If you press **Enter** before you notice the mistake, you can press **Esc** to try to stop the command before it is carried out.

Case doesn't matter when you type a command; you can type the command in uppercase or lowercase letters. PC DOS reads *COPY*, *copy*, and *Copy* as the same command.

Chapter 2

Making PC DOS Work

On your desk, you now have a complete personal computer system ready for use. You know what all the hardware and software components can do, and you are ready to get to work.

Wouldn't you like to be able to just sit down in front of your computer and say, "Start up, and load Word for Windows so that I can create a document in a directory called Winword Docs," and have the computer respond? But you can't. That's why you need PC DOS.

In this chapter, you learn to use PC DOS to put your computer to work. You learn to use basic commands to manage disks, files, and directories.

Starting PC DOS

Cold boot

To turn on your computer by using the power switch.

PC DOS starts automatically when you start, or boot, your computer. If your computer is off, you start it by using a *cold boot*. To cold boot your computer, press the On/Off switch into the On position. Look for the On/Off switch on the front of your computer. Your display probably has a separate On/Off switch; if so, you must turn this switch to On as well.

As soon as you turn on your computer, it begins running a Power-On Self Test (POST) to make sure that all components are working properly. You probably will hear sounds and see information on-screen as the system starts. Some computers count the available memory during the POST and display the amount in a message on-screen, as in the following:

```
003712 KB
OK Wait
```

If you have problems...

If you see the following message, your computer cannot find PC DOS:

```
Non-system disk or disk error

Replace and strike any key when ready
```

If PC DOS is installed on the hard disk, make sure that drive A does not have a diskette inserted in it. Press any key to try loading PC DOS again. You must install PC DOS before you can use your computer.

When the POST is complete, PC DOS starts. It carries out the commands in the CONFIG.SYS file, and then it carries out the commands in the AUTOEXEC.BAT file. (For more information on CONFIG.SYS and AUTOEXEC.BAT, see Chapter 1, "Understanding System Basics," and Chapter 8, "Configuring Your Personal Computer.") As PC DOS starts, you probably will see an on-screen message similar to the following one, indicating that PC DOS is loading into memory, as well as other messages as PC DOS carries out the commands in the CONFIG.SYS and AUTOEXEC.BAT files:

```
Starting PC DOS...

Microsoft (R) Mouse Driver Version 8.20
Copyright  Microsoft Corp. 1983-1992.
Copyright  IBM Corp. 1992-1993
Mouse driver installed.
```

On some systems, PC DOS may prompt you to enter the date and time during start-up. To enter the date, follow these steps:

1. Type the current date, using the format indicated within the parentheses on the command line.

2. Press **Enter**.

When PC DOS prompts you for the date, it also prompts you for the time. To enter the time, follow these steps:

1. Type the current time, using the format indicated within the parentheses on the command line.

2. Press **Enter**.

Note: *For more information on setting the date and time, see the section "Setting the Date and Time," later in this chapter.*

When you have successfully loaded PC DOS, the following PC DOS command prompt appears on-screen:

```
c:\>
```

Usually, the PC DOS command prompt displays the current drive (C:), the current directory (\), and the prompt symbol (>), but the prompt can appear differently on your computer. For information on changing the appearance of the PC DOS command prompt, see the section "Changing the PC DOS Command Prompt," later in this chapter.

2

If you have problems...

If someone added a command to your AUTOEXEC.BAT file to display something other than the PC DOS command prompt, you may see something different on-screen when PC DOS starts. For example, your computer may display the PC DOS Shell, or Windows, or a customized menu screen. For information on what to do when your computer displays the PC DOS Shell, see Chapter 1, "Understanding System Basics." For information on what to do when your computer displays Windows, see Chapter 3, "Working with the Windows Desktop." For information on what to do if your computer displays a customized menu, consult the documentation that came with the application program, or contact your company's support staff.

Restarting PC DOS

Warm boot
The restarting of your computer without turning off the power.

When necessary, you can use a *warm boot* to restart PC DOS without turning your computer off and then on again. A warm boot is faster than a cold boot and saves wear and tear on your hardware.

Caution
Restart PC DOS only if your system will not respond to commands. Restarting PC DOS without exiting all application programs can damage files and data.

To perform a warm boot, follow these steps:

1. Press and hold down **Ctrl**.

2. While still holding down **Ctrl**, press and hold down **Alt**.

3. While still holding down **Ctrl** and **Alt**, press and hold down **Del**.

4. Release all three keys at the same time. The computer skips the POST and immediately loads PC DOS.

If you have problems...	If nothing happens when you release the keys, try pressing and releasing **Ctrl+Alt+Del** again. If nothing happens, turn off your computer. Wait a minute or so before you turn it on again.

Some computers also have a Reset button. Pressing the Reset button is the same as performing a warm boot.

Turning Off Your Computer

You should turn off the computer only when you are at a PC DOS command prompt and you already have closed all other application programs, including Windows. When you are working in an application program, save all files and exit the program before you turn off the computer.

To turn off your computer, follow these steps:

1. Locate the power switch on your computer.

2. Gently press the power switch into the Off position.

3. When necessary, turn off your display as well.

Changing the PC DOS Command Prompt

By default, the PC DOS command prompt displays the current drive, directory, and the prompt symbol (>). You can modify the appearance of the prompt by using the PROMPT command.

To change the appearance of the prompt to include the current date, follow these steps:

1. Type **PROMPT**.

2. Press the **spacebar** once to insert a space between the PROMPT command and the description of the type of prompt you want.

3. Type **PD$G**. This identifies a prompt that includes the current directory.

4. Press **Enter**. PC DOS changes the prompt to include the current directory, which should look like the following:

```
C:\Thurs 05-18-1995>
```

This prompt includes the symbols for the current drive (C:), the current directory (\), the current date (Thurs 05-18-1995), and the prompt symbol (>).

Using the Online Book Viewer

PC DOS 7 comes with an on-line book viewer that you can use to read documentation stored in files on your computer. The book viewer is a useful learning and reference tool, because you can quickly look up information you need without leaving your computer. You also can use the viewer to print text from the online books, or to copy the information from the book into a text file.

You can use the book viewer to read most files with the extension INF. PC DOS 7 comes with three on-line books:

CMDREF	This is the PC DOS Command Reference. It contains information about PC DOS commands, device drivers, and INI files.
DOSREXX	This is the documentation for using the REXX programming language. It contains the basic information you need to know for getting started with REXX.
DOSERROR	This is a guide to common error messages. It contains a list of error messages you might encounter while using DOS or the optional DOS tools.

Note: *You can use the online book viewer from DOS or from Windows. If you install at least one optional tool for Windows when you install PC DOS, icons for starting the online books appear in the PC DOS Tools group. For information on starting a program in Windows, see Chapter 4, "Making Windows Work."*

To start the PC DOS book viewer when you do not know which book you want to open, follow these steps:

1. At the PC DOS command prompt, type **VIEW**.

Use the VIEW
command to start
the document
viewer.

Type the
command

2. Press **Enter**.

The PC DOS viewer opens to display the Select a File menu of files with
the INF extensionin the current directory. To open one of the files from
the list, use the up and down arrow keys to highlight the file name, then
press Enter. If you have a mouse, you can just double-click the file name.

**If you have
problems...**

The viewer cannot read *all* files with the INF extension. There may be some
files that appear in the viewer main menu that cannot be opened.

Viewer menu bar

You can use the
PC DOS viewer to
open documenta-
tion on-line.

Choose a book
to view

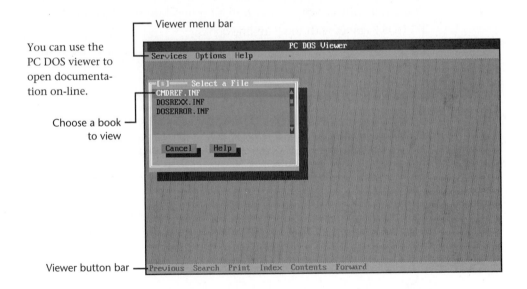

Viewer button bar

If you know the name of the book you want to open, you can open it
directly from the PC DOS command prompt, without using the Select a
File menu in the viewer.

To open a book directly from the PC DOS command prompt, follow these steps:

1. At the PC DOS command prompt, type **VIEW**.

2. Press the **spacebar** one time to leave a space between the VIEW command and the file name of the book you want to open.

3. Type the name of the book, as in the following:

   ```
   C:\>VIEW CMDREF
   ```

4. Press **Enter**. PC DOS opens the viewer and displays the table of contents for the book you specified—in this case, the Command Reference.

You can choose a topic from the book's table of contents to get more information.

Double-click a topic to display it

Click a plus sign to display additional topics

```
                        PC DOS 7 Command Reference
  Services  Options  Help

                            = Contents =                        [ ]
   [+] Using the Online Viewer (PC DOS Viewer)
   [+] About This Book
   [+] What's New for PC DOS 7
   [+] Command-Line Basics
   [+] Command Descriptions
       Command Type Tables - Introduction
       Batch Commands Quick Reference Table
       CONFIG.SYS Commands Quick Reference Table
       Device Driver Commands Quick Reference Table
       Stacker Compression Commands Quick Reference Tab
   [+] Customizing Keyboards for International Use
   [+] DOS Commands in Alphabetic Order
   [+] Configuring .INI Files


  Previous  Search  Print  Index  Contents  Forward
```

Moving around in the PC DOS Viewer

You probably have noticed that the book viewer does not look anything like DOS. That is because it has its own interface, similar to the PC DOS Shell and some of the DOS tools you learn about in Chapter 10, "Using PC DOS 7.0 Tools."

To use the viewer, you make selections from menus with a mouse or with the keyboard. You do not have to type commands.

The viewer uses a graphical user interface to make it easy for you to find what you need. Use the keyboard or the mouse to navigate through the on-line books.

Click to open the Services menu

```
                    PC DOS 7 Command Reference
  Services  Options  Help
[•]========= What's New for PC DOS ? =========

 PC DOS 7 includes the following new features as well as enhancements to
 features in prior versions of PC DOS:

 o PC DOS Setup program includes the following enhancements that allows
   you to:

     - Use a mouse device during installation.
     - Use the DOSKey program immediately after installing DOS, because
       the DOSKEY command-line statement is now automatically added to
       your AUTOEXEC.BAT file.
     - View or edit the changes Setup made to your CONFIG.SYS and
       AUTOEXEC.BAT files prior to system restart.  For example, if you
       use another command retrieval program other than DOSKEY, you can
       edit the AUTOEXEC.BAT file and delete this command-line statement
       before the Setup changes become effective.
     - Understand what changes were made to these system files by
       reviewing comment lines added by Setup.  Comment lines describe
       what was added in these files or what was replaced, updated, or

 Previous  Search  Print  Index  Contents  Forward
```

Click to page up

Click to display table of contents

Click to page down

To select an option from the menu bar at the top of the screen or from the button bar at the bottom of the screen, click it with a mouse. Using the keyboard, press and hold down the **Alt** key; then press the highlighted letter in the option name. Table 2.1 describes the options on the viewer button bar. Table 2.2 describes the options on the viewer menu bar.

When you select an option from the menu bar, a drop-down menu opens on-screen. To select a command from a drop-down menu, click the command name with the mouse, or press the highlighted letter in the command name.

To select an option from a menu list, such as a topic from the table of contents that appears when you first open a book, double-click the option with a mouse or use the up- and down-arrow keys to highlight the option and press Enter.

If a topic in the table of contents has subtopics, you see a plus sign (+) to the left of the topic. Click the plus sign to display the subtopics; this is called *expanding the topics*. Click the minus sign to hide the subtopics; this is called *collapsing the topics*.

To move up or down the text displayed on your screen, click the scroll arrows at the right side of the screen, or use the PgUp and PgDn keys on your keyboard.

Table 2.1 Viewer Button Bar Options

Option	Function
Previous	Goes back to the previously displayed topic. This option is dimmed if you have not opened another topic.
Search	Opens a Search dialog box where you can enter a specific word for which you would like to view information. You can type a command name, for example, to view the information about that command in the Command Reference on-line book.
Print	Prints the topic currently displayed on your screen.
Index	Displays an index of topics for the on-line book. You can choose a topic to view from the index.
Contents	Displays the table of contents for the on-line book. You can choose a topic to view from the table of contents.
Forward	Pages forward through the book from topic to topic. This option is dimmed if no topic is open in the viewer.

Table 2.2 Viewer Menu Commands

Command	Function
Services	Opens the Services menu from which you can choose to search for a topic, print a topic, copy a topic to a text file, append a topic to a text file, or exit the viewer.
Options	Opens the Options menu from which you can choose to expand or collapse the table of contents topics, view the table of contents, view the index, or return to the previously displayed topic.
Help	Opens the Help menu from which you can choose Help information about using the on-line book viewer.

Exiting from the PC DOS Viewer

To exit from the PC DOS viewer and return to the PC DOS command prompt, follow these steps:

1. Choose Ser**v**ices or press **Alt+V** to open the Services menu.

2. Choose E**x**it or press **X** to close the Viewer.

Use the Services
menu to close the
viewer and return
to the PC DOS
command prompt.

Click to close
the viewer

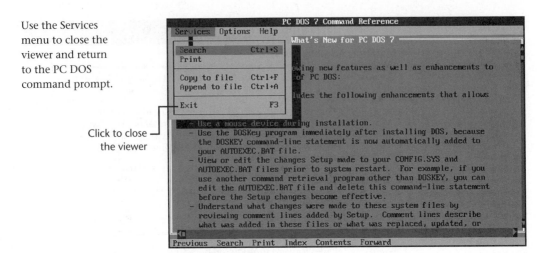

Using the Viewer to Get Online Help

Whenever you are working with PC DOS 7.0, you can use the viewer to
display Help about any command or error message. This feature is useful
when you forget which command you should use to accomplish a specific task or when you need additional information about how to type a
command correctly.

To display information about a particular PC DOS 7.0 command, follow
these steps:

1. At the PC DOS command prompt, type **HELP**.

2. Press the **spacebar** once to leave a space between the HELP
   command and the name of the command about which you need
   information.

3. Type the name of the command about which you need information, as in the following:

   C:\>HELP **PROMPT**

4. Press **Enter**. PC DOS 7.0 displays information about how to use the
   specified command.

Use the Help command to go directly to the page in the Command Reference on-line book that describes the command you want to learn about.

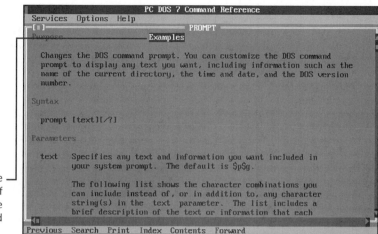

Click to see examples of how to use the command

To get help about a specific PC DOS error message, follow these steps:

1. At the PC DOS command prompt, type **HELP**.

2. Press the **spacebar** once to leave a space between the HELP command and the first letter of the error message.

3. Type the first letter of the error message.

4. Press **Enter**. PC DOS 7.0 opens the Command Reference on-line book to an alphabetical list of error messages. Press PgUp or PgDn or click the scroll arrows to move through the documentation to find the message you need.

Scroll through the Command Reference on-line book to get help about error messages.

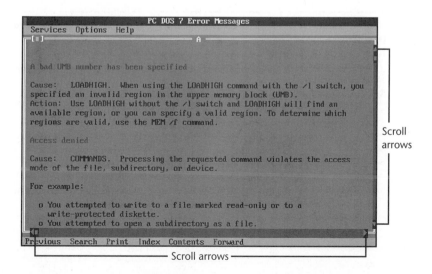

Scroll arrows

Scroll arrows

Note: *If you use a version of PC DOS prior to 7.0, you can use the HELP command alone to display a list of all PC DOS commands. Just type* **HELP** *at the PC DOS command prompt and press* **Enter***. PC DOS displays an alphabetical list of commands, along with brief descriptions of what each command does.*

Making a Directory

By using directories, you and PC DOS can keep your files organized. The logical way PC DOS arranges directories and files on a disk always enables you to locate the files you need. (For information about how PC DOS organizes stored data, see Chapter 1, "Understanding System Basics.")

To make a directory, follow these steps:

1. At the PC DOS command prompt, type **MD**—the command for making a directory.

2. Type the path, followed by the name of the directory you want PC DOS to make, as in the following:

    C:\>MD\DATA

    The C:\> is the PC DOS command prompt, the MD is the Make Directory command, the \ is the current directory, and DATA is the new directory name—a subdirectory of the root directory.

3. Press **Enter**. PC DOS makes the directory.

If you have problems...

If you cannot find the directory you just made, you may have typed the wrong path.

If you do not type the entire path to the new directory, PC DOS makes the directory a subdirectory of the current directory.

Changing Directories

Unless you specify otherwise, PC DOS carries out commands on the *current directory*.

**Current
directory**
The directory PC
DOS currently is
working in.

You can specify a directory every time you type a command, or you can change to the directory you want to make current. The command to change the current directory is a useful one, because you can use it to navigate around the directory structure by moving from directory to directory.

To change directories, follow these steps:

1. At the PC DOS command prompt, type **CD**—the command for changing the current directory.

2. Type the path to the directory you want to make current.

3. Press **Enter**. PC DOS makes the specified directory the current directory. When your prompt is set to display the current directory, you see the directory name in the prompt:

   ```
   C:\>CD\DATA
   C:\DATA>
   ```

   The PC DOS command prompt indicates that \DATA is now the current directory.

**If you have
problems...**

If you see the message `Invalid directory`, check your typing to make sure that you have spelled the directory name correctly. You may have tried to change to a directory that does not exist. You must create the directory before you can change to it. See the preceding section, "Making a Directory."

If you are in the current directory and you want to maintain files and disks, issue commands, and start application programs in that directory, you do not have to specify a directory path each time you type the command.

Note: *To change to the root directory from any other directory, type **CD**, and then press **Enter**.*

Removing a Directory

It is important to keep your disk free of old and unused files and directories. Unused directories take up valuable disk space. If you accidentally make a directory or have an old directory you no longer need, you can remove it from your disk.

Note: *You can use the RD (Remove Directory) command only to remove an empty directory. If the directory contains files or subdirectories that you want to remove, you must delete them first, or use the DELTREE command. Use the RD command to delete subdirectories. Use the DEL command to delete files. For information on deleting files, see the section "Deleting Files," later in this chapter.*

To remove a directory, follow these steps:

1. Change to the directory that contains the directory you want to remove.

2. Type **RD**, the command for removing a directory, followed by the path and the name of the directory you want to remove:

    C:\>RD DATA

3. Press **Enter**. PC DOS removes the directory.

If you have problems...

If you see the message `Invalid path, not directory`, or `directory not empty`, you have mistyped the path or directory name, or there still are files or subdirectories in the directory.

Displaying the Contents of a Directory

You can use PC DOS to display a list of files and directories contained on any disk or in any directory.

To display a list of all files and directories in the current directory, follow these steps:

1. Change to the directory you want to make current.

2. At the PC DOS command prompt, type **DIR**—the command for displaying files and directories.

3. Press **Enter**. PC DOS displays a list of the files and directories in the current directory.

Notice that the following information appears on-screen:

Information Provided in Column	Description
File name	The root of the file name (up to eight charac- ters) appears first.
Extension	The extension is listed in the second column.
Directory	If the entry is a directory, you see <DIR> in the third column.
File Size	The fourth column lists the size of the file. The size is measured in bytes. One byte equals about one character. If the entry is a directory, nothing is listed.
Date	The fifth column displays the date when the file was created or modified.
Time	The final column displays the time when the file was created or modified.

The two lines at the end of the directory listing display the number of files, bytes used, and bytes free (disk space remaining). The PC DOS command prompt appears at the bottom of the listing so that you can type the next command.

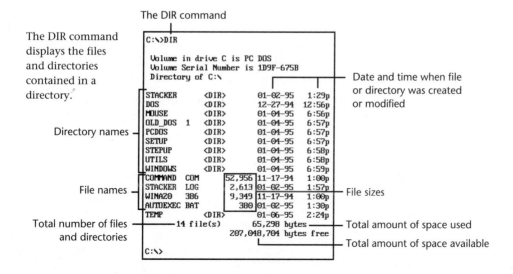

The DIR command

The DIR command displays the files and directories contained in a directory.

Directory names

File names

Total number of files and directories

Date and time when file or directory was created or modified

File sizes

Total amount of space used

Total amount of space available

```
C:\>DIR

 Volume in drive C is PC DOS
 Volume Serial Number is 1D9F-675B
 Directory of C:\

STACKER      <DIR>      01-02-95   1:29p
DOS          <DIR>      12-27-94  12:56p
MOUSE        <DIR>      01-04-95   6:56p
OLD_DOS   1  <DIR>      01-04-95   6:57p
PCDOS        <DIR>      01-04-95   6:57p
SETUP        <DIR>      01-04-95   6:57p
STEPUP       <DIR>      01-04-95   6:58p
UTILS        <DIR>      01-04-95   6:58p
WINDOWS      <DIR>      01-04-95   6:59p
COMMAND  COM    52,956  11-17-94   1:00p
STACKER  LOG     2,613  01-02-95   1:57p
WINA20   386     9,349  11-17-94   1:00p
AUTOEXEC BAT       380  01-02-95   1:30p
TEMP         <DIR>      01-06-95   2:24p
        14 file(s)      65,298 bytes
                    207,048,704 bytes free
C:\>
```

Modifying a Directory List

You can modify the way PC DOS lists the contents of a directory on-screen by adding *switches* and *parameters* to the DIR command.

Changing the appearance of the listing is useful when you have too many files to display on one screen, when you need to display only certain files, or when you want to display only certain information about the files. (For more information about using the DIR command, type **HELP DIR** at the PC DOS command prompt and press **Enter**.)

Displaying a Wide File Listing

When you want to see more of the contents of a large disk or directory on-screen at one time, you can add a switch to the DIR command to tell PC DOS to display a wide file listing.

A wide file listing shows multiple columns of file and directory names. It does not display any additional information.

To display a wide file listing, follow these steps:

1. At the PC DOS command prompt, type **DIR**.

2. Type **/W**, the switch that tells PC DOS to display a wide file listing. (The W can be uppercase or lowercase.)

3. Press **Enter**. PC DOS displays a wide file listing of the current directory.

Notice that only file and directory names are listed in five columns across the screen. The other file information (size, date, and time) does not appear. Directories appear in brackets, and the last two lines of the listing display the number of files, number of bytes used, and number of bytes free.

Type the command and the command switch here

In a wide file
listing, only the
file or directory
name is displayed.

Directory names are
enclosed in brackets

File names have
extensions

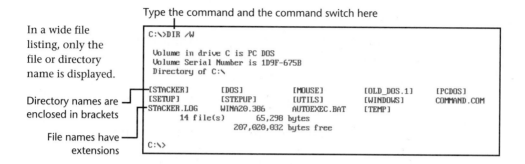

```
C:\>DIR /W

 Volume in drive C is PC DOS
 Volume Serial Number is 1D9F-675B
 Directory of C:\

[STACKER]        [DOS]            [MOUSE]           [OLD_DOS.1]      [PCDOS]
[SETUP]          [STEPUP]         [UTILS]           [WINDOWS]        COMMAND.COM
STACKER.LOG      WINA20.386       AUTOEXEC.BAT      [TEMP]
        14 file(s)         65,298 bytes
                      207,020,032 bytes free

C:\>
```

Displaying a Directory List One Page at a Time

When the directory contains many files and directories, you can tell PC
DOS to display only one page at a time. PC DOS pauses until you tell it
to display the next page, giving you a chance to read the list.

To display a directory list one page at a time, follow these steps:

1. Change to the directory you want to list.

2. At the PC DOS command prompt, type **DIR**.

3. Type **/P**, the switch that tells PC DOS to pause between pages in a
directory listing.

4. Press **Enter**. PC DOS displays the first page of files.

5. Press any key when you are ready to display the next page.

When you use the
/P switch with the
DIR command, PC
DOS pauses at the
bottom of the page
until you press any
key to continue.

```
 Volume in drive C is PC DOS
 Volume Serial Number is 1D9F-675B
 Directory of C:\

STACKER        <DIR>         01-02-95    1:29p
DOS            <DIR>         12-27-94   12:56p
MOUSE          <DIR>         01-04-95    6:56p
OLD_DOS   1    <DIR>         01-04-95    6:57p
PCDOS          <DIR>         01-04-95    6:57p
SETUP          <DIR>         01-04-95    6:57p
STEPUP         <DIR>         01-04-95    6:58p
UTILS          <DIR>         01-04-95    6:58p
WINDOWS        <DIR>         01-04-95    6:59p
COMMAND   COM        52,956 11-17-94    1:00p
STACKER   LOG         2,613 01-02-95    1:57p
CONFIG    SYS           351 01-04-95    6:26p
DATA           <DIR>         01-06-95    2:38p
WINA20    386         9,349 11-17-94    1:00p
MSOFFICE       <DIR>         01-06-95    2:38p
AUTOEXEC  BAT           380 01-02-95    1:30p
CONFIG    CPS           211 01-02-95    1:36p
TEST           <DIR>         01-06-95    2:40p
TEMP           <DIR>         01-06-95    2:24p
Press any key to continue . . .
```

2

Listing Selected Files

You can use PC DOS wild-card characters to display only selected files in a directory listing. For information about wild-card characters, see Chapter 1, "Understanding System Basics."

To display only selected files, follow these steps:

1. Change to the directory you want to make current.

2. At the PC DOS command prompt, type **DIR**.

3. Press the **spacebar** once to leave a space between the command name and the parameter you are about to type.

4. Specify the files you want to list by using wild-card characters:

   ■ Use * in place of any one character, and any character that follows it. Type ***.DOC** to list all files with the extension DOC, for example.

   ■ Use ? in place of any one character. Type **?FILE.DOC** to list files that begin with any character, followed by FILE.DOC, for example. This would include 1FILE.DOC, 2FILE.DOC, and so on—but not 10FILE.DOC. (Type **??FILE.DOC** to get 10FILE.DOC.)

5. Press **Enter**. PC DOS displays a list of all files that match the file specification you entered on the command line.

Type the file
specification

PC DOS lists all
files in the
\TEMP\TEST
directory that
match the file
specification
*.DOC

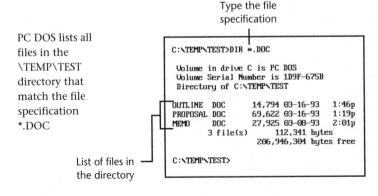

```
C:\TEMP\TEST>DIR *.DOC

Volume in drive C is PC DOS
Volume Serial Number is 1D9F-675B
Directory of C:\TEMP\TEST

OUTLINE  DOC      14,794 03-16-93   1:46p
PROPOSAL DOC      69,622 03-16-93   1:19p
MEMO     DOC      27,925 03-08-93   2:01p
        3 file(s)      112,341 bytes
                   206,946,304 bytes free

C:\TEMP\TEST>
```

List of files in
the directory

Listing Directories in a Tree Diagram

You can display a tree diagram of directories and subdirectories by using the TREE command.

To display a tree diagram of directories, follow these steps:

1. Change to the directory you want to make current.

2. At the PC DOS command prompt, type **TREE**.

3. Press **Enter**. PC DOS displays a tree diagram of all directories in the current directory, and their subdirectories.

By using the TREE command, you can see on-screen the relationship between directories.

Directory tree

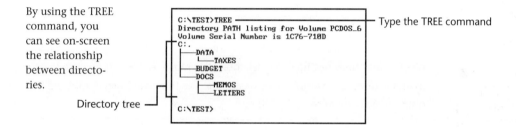

```
C:\TEST>TREE
Directory PATH listing for Volume PCDOS_6
Volume Serial Number is 1C76-718D
C:.
├──DATA
│   └──TAXES
├──BUDGET
└──DOCS
    ├──MEMOS
    └──LETTERS

C:\TEST>
```

Type the TREE command

Clearing the Screen

Sometimes the PC DOS screen can become cluttered with information. You can use the CLS (Clear Screen) command to clear all information from the screen except the PC DOS command prompt.

To clear the screen, follow these steps:

1. At the PC DOS command prompt, type **CLS**.

2. Press **Enter**. PC DOS displays the PC DOS command prompt at the top of an empty screen.

Inserting Diskettes

To transfer data into and to take data from your computer, you can use diskettes. When handling diskettes, you must be careful not to damage them. (For information about diskettes and disk types, see Chapter 1, "Understanding System Basics.")

To insert a diskette into a diskette drive, follow these steps:

1. Hold the diskette so that the label is facing up.

2. Gently insert the diskette into the drive, and then take one of the following actions:

   ■ When you are using a 5 1/4-inch diskette, you must shut the drive door. Push the lever so that it is closed.

   ■ When you are using a 3 1/2-inch diskette, you should hear a click, indicating that the diskette is inserted. The eject button pops out.

If you have problems...

If you are using a 5 1/4-inch diskette that doesn't have a label, hold the diskette so that the notched side is on the left. If you are using a 3 1/2-inch diskette that does not have a label, look for writing (diskette type, arrow, or manufacturer, for example) to indicate the side that should face up. Hold the diskette so that you see the writing.

Changing the Current Drive

Current drive
The drive on which PC DOS is working.

Unless otherwise specified, PC DOS carries out all commands on the *current drive*.

You can change the current drive so that you do not have to specify a different drive every time you type a command.

To change the current drive, follow these steps:

1. Insert a diskette into the drive you want to make current.

2. At the PC DOS command prompt, type the letter of the drive you want to make current.

3. Immediately to the right of the drive letter, type a colon (:).
   For drive A, the command line should look like the following:

   ```
   C:\>A:
   ```

4. Press **Enter**.

5. PC DOS makes the specified drive the current drive. The PC DOS command prompt changes to show the current drive:

A:\>

If you have problems...

If you see an error message similar to the following, you have not inserted a diskette into the drive you want to make current or you inserted an unformatted diskette:

```
Not ready reading drive A
Abort, Retry, Fail?
```

Insert a diskette and press **R** to try again.

Formatting a Diskette

Before you can store information on a diskette, it must be formatted. Formatting prepares the diskette so that PC DOS can write information on it and then find the information when it is needed.

Note: *Formatting erases all information from a diskette. Make sure that the diskette you are formatting is blank or that you do not need the existing files.*

Caution

Do not use the FORMAT command on your hard disk. Formatting erases all data on the disk.

To format a diskette, follow these steps:

1. Insert a blank diskette into the drive—either A or B—that you want to use. To see whether anything is on the diskette, use the DIR command.

2. At the PC DOS command prompt, type **FORMAT**.

3. Press the **spacebar** once.

4. Type the letter of the drive you are using, and then type a colon.

5. Press **Enter**.

6. PC DOS prompts you to insert a new diskette into the specified drive, even if you already have done so.

7. Make sure that the diskette you want to format is correctly inserted in the drive, and then press **Enter**.

FORMAT checks the existing disk format. If that format differs from the one being requested, FORMAT prompts you to confirm the procedure.

Volume Label
A name for a diskette.

8. When the format is complete, PC DOS prompts you to enter a *volume label*. If the prompt appears, type the label and press **Enter**; or, just press **Enter** if you don't want to have a volume label.

9. PC DOS displays information about the diskette just formatted and then asks whether you want to format another. Press **Y** to format another diskette. Press **N** to return to the PC DOS command prompt.

Formatting erases all existing data from the diskette. Make sure that the diskette is blank or that you do not need the data anymore.

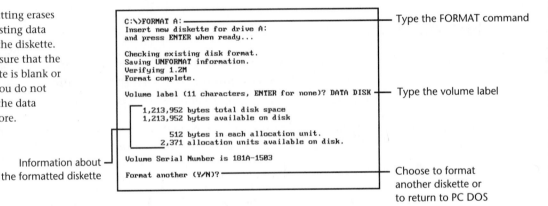

Type the FORMAT command

Type the volume label

Information about the formatted diskette

Choose to format another diskette or to return to PC DOS

Changing a Volume Label

You can change a volume label any time after a diskette has been formatted without affecting the data stored on the diskette.

To view the current volume label, follow these steps:

1. If necessary, insert the diskette into the diskette drive.

2. Make the drive that contains the diskette the current drive.

3. At the PC DOS command prompt, type **VOL**.

4. Press **Enter**. PC DOS displays the volume label and the volume serial number.

Use the VOL
command to
display the label of
the diskette in the
current drive.

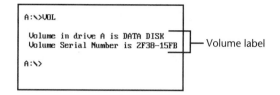
— Volume label

To change the volume label, follow these steps:

1. If necessary, insert the diskette into the diskette drive.

2. Make the drive that contains the diskette the current drive.

3. At the PC DOS command prompt, type **LABEL**.

Use the LABEL
command to
change the label of
the diskette in the
current drive.

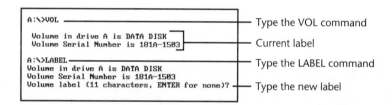

- Type the VOL command
- Current label
- Type the LABEL command
- Type the new label

4. Press **Enter**. PC DOS displays the current volume label and the
volume serial number and prompts you to enter a new label.

5. Type the new label.

6. Press **Enter**. PC DOS changes the label. Use the VOL command to
view the new label name.

Copying a Diskette

You can copy the entire contents of one diskette to another diskette of
the same size and capacity by using the DISKCOPY command. (For information about diskette sizes and capacities, see Chapter 1, "Understanding System Basics.")

Copying diskettes is easier when you have two diskette drives of the same
size, but you can copy a diskette using one drive as well.

Note: *DISKCOPY copies everything from the old diskette to the new diskette. If
the diskette you are copying has errors, the errors are copied to the new diskette
as well.*

Copying a Diskette Using Two Diskette Drives

In order to copy a diskette using two diskette drives, the drives must be the same size. Therefore, you must have two 5 1/4-inch drives or two 3 1/2-inch drives.

To copy a diskette using two diskette drives of equal size, follow these steps:

Source diskette
The diskette that contains the information you want to copy.

Target diskette
The diskette to which you want to copy the information.

1. Insert the *source diskette* into drive A.

2. Insert the *target diskette* into drive B.

3. At the PC DOS command prompt, type **DISKCOPY**.

4. Press the **spacebar** once.

5. Type **A:.**

6. Press the **spacebar** once.

7. Type **B:.**

8. Press **Enter**.

9. PC DOS prompts you to insert the source and target diskettes into the correct drives, even if you already have done so.

You can easily copy from one diskette to another using two diskette drives of equal size.

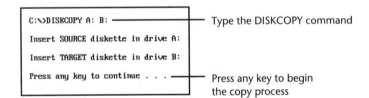

C:\>DISKCOPY A: B: ——————— Type the DISKCOPY command

Insert SOURCE diskette in drive A:

Insert TARGET diskette in drive B:

Press any key to continue . . . —————— Press any key to begin the copy process

10. Press any key to continue. PC DOS begins copying the diskette.

11. When PC DOS finishes copying the diskette, it asks whether you want to copy another one. If you want to copy another diskette, press **Y** and then **Enter**. If you want to return to the PC DOS command prompt, press **N** and then **Enter**.

If you have problems...

If you see the following message, you tried to use two drives or two diskettes that are not the same size or capacity:

```
Drive types or diskette types not compatible
Copy process ended
```

Use the procedure described in the next section to copy a diskette using only one drive.

Copying a Diskette Using One Diskette Drive

Even if you have only one diskette drive or two diskette drives of different sizes, you can use the DISKCOPY command to copy a diskette.

To copy a diskette using a single diskette drive, follow these steps:

1. Insert the source diskette into drive A.

2. At the PC DOS command prompt, type **DISKCOPY**.

3. Press the **spacebar** once.

4. Type **A:**.

5. Press the **spacebar** once.

6. Type **A:**.

7. Press **Enter**. PC DOS prompts you to insert the source diskette into drive A.

8. Press any key to begin the copy process.

9. PC DOS prompts you to insert the target diskette into drive A. Remove the source diskette, and insert the target diskette.

   PC DOS prompts you each time you need to swap the diskettes in drive A. Depending on how many bytes the diskette holds and the amount of memory on your computer, you may have to swap diskettes several times.

10. When the diskette has been copied completely, PC DOS asks whether you want to copy another one. If you want to copy another diskette, press **Y** and then press **Enter**. If you want to return to the PC DOS command prompt, press **N** and then press **Enter**.

Displaying the Contents of a File

You can view the contents of a file without affecting the file by using the TYPE command.

To display the contents of a file, follow these steps:

1. Change to the directory that contains the file you want to display.

2. At the PC DOS command prompt, type the word **TYPE**.

3. Press the **spacebar** once.

4. Type the name of the file that you want to display.

5. Press **Enter**. PC DOS displays the contents of the file on-screen.

Type the command

PC DOS displays
the contents of the
AUTOEXEC.BAT
file.

Contents of the file —

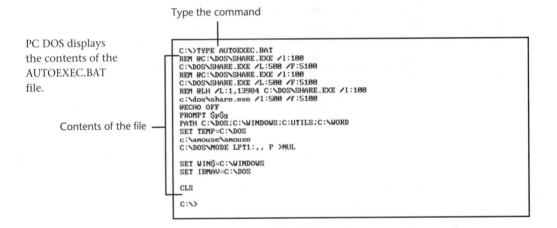

```
C:\>TYPE AUTOEXEC.BAT
REM @C:\DOS\SHARE.EXE /1:100
C:\DOS\SHARE.EXE /L:500 /F:5100
REM @C:\DOS\SHARE.EXE /1:100
C:\DOS\SHARE.EXE /L:500 /F:5100
REM @LH /L:1,13984 C:\DOS\SHARE.EXE /1:100
c:\dos\share.exe /1:500 /f:5100
@ECHO OFF
PROMPT $p$g
PATH C:\DOS;C:\WINDOWS;C:\UTILS;C:\WORD
SET TEMP=C:\DOS
c:\amouse\amouse
C:\DOS\MODE LPT1:,, P >NUL

SET WIN$=C:\WINDOWS
SET IBMAV=C:\DOS

CLS

C:\>
```

For information on editing a file, see Chapter 7, "Working with the Text Editor."

Copying a File

With PC DOS, you quickly can make copies of existing files. You can copy a file to the same directory, from one directory to another, or from one disk to another. You even can copy groups of files at the same time.

Note: *After you copy a file to a disk, you can take it to another computer, or you can keep it in a safe place to use as a backup.*

Copying a File to the Same Directory

To copy a file to the same directory, follow these steps:

1. Change to the directory that contains the file you want to copy.

2. At the PC DOS command prompt, type **COPY**.

3. Press the **spacebar** once.

4. Type the name of the file you want to copy.

5. Press the **spacebar** once.

6. Type the name you want to assign to the copy of the file.
The command should look like the following:

```
C:\>COPY AUTOEXEC.BAT AUTOEXEC.OLD
```

7. Press **Enter**. PC DOS copies the file and displays the message

```
1 file(s) copied
```

Now there are two copies of the same file in the current directory. One
copy is named AUTOEXEC.BAT, and one is named AUTOEXEC.OLD.
You have two versions of the same file, but they have different names.

Copying a File to a Different Directory or Drive

To copy a file to a different directory or drive, follow these steps:

1. Change to the directory that contains the file you want to copy.

2. At the PC DOS command prompt, type **COPY**.

3. Press the **spacebar** once.

4. Type the name of the file you want to copy.

5. Press the **spacebar** once.

6. Type the path to the location where you want to store the copy.
Include a drive letter, if necessary. The command should look like
the following:

```
C:\>COPY AUTOEXEC.BAT C:\TEST\DATA
```

Because you are using the same file name, you do not have to type
it after the new location name.

7. Press **Enter**. PC DOS copies the file and displays the message

```
1 file(s) copied
```

The original AUTOEXEC.BAT file is still in the root directory, and a copy of the AUTOEXEC.BAT file is in the C:\TEST\DATA subdirectory.

Copying a Group of Files to Another Location

To copy a group of files to another drive or directory, follow these steps:

1. Change to the directory that contains the files you want to copy.

2. At the PC DOS command prompt, type **COPY**.

3. Press the **spacebar** once.

4. Using wild-card characters, type the file specification for the group of files you want to copy. Type ***.DOC** to copy all files with the extension DOC, or type ***.*** to copy all files, for example.

5. Press the **spacebar** once.

6. Type the path to the location where you want to store the copied files.

7. Press **Enter**. PC DOS copies all the files that match the file specification to the new location and displays the name of each file as it is copied.

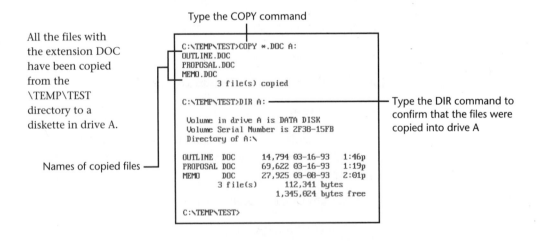

Type the COPY command

All the files with the extension DOC have been copied from the \TEMP\TEST directory to a diskette in drive A.

Names of copied files

```
C:\TEMP\TEST>COPY *.DOC A:
OUTLINE.DOC
PROPOSAL.DOC
MEMO.DOC
        3 file(s) copied

C:\TEMP\TEST>DIR A:

 Volume in drive A is DATA DISK
 Volume Serial Number is 2F3B-15FB
 Directory of A:\

OUTLINE  DOC     14,794 03-16-93   1:46p
PROPOSAL DOC     69,622 03-16-93   1:19p
MEMO     DOC     27,925 03-08-93   2:01p
        3 file(s)      112,341 bytes
                     1,345,024 bytes free

C:\TEMP\TEST>
```

Type the DIR command to confirm that the files were copied into drive A

Renaming a File

You can use PC DOS to rename an existing file, without affecting the contents of the file.

To rename a file, follow these steps:

1. Change to the directory that contains the file you want to rename.

2. At the PC DOS command prompt, type **RENAME**.

3. Press the **spacebar** once.

4. Type the current name of the file you want to rename. To rename a group of files, use the wild-card characters.

5. Press the **spacebar** once.

6. Type the new name you want to give to the file.

7. Press **Enter**. PC DOS renames the file.

Deleting Files

When you no longer need a file, you can delete it so that it doesn't take up valuable disk space. You can delete one file, or you can use wild-card characters to specify a group of files to delete.

Note: *Before you delete a file, you should make sure that the file does not contain data that you need.*

To delete a file, follow these steps:

1. Change to the directory that contains the file you want to delete.

2. At the PC DOS command prompt, type **DEL**.

3. Press the **spacebar** once.

4. Type the name of the file you want to delete. To delete a group of files, type the file specification, using wild-card characters.

5. Press **Enter**. PC DOS deletes the specified file.

If you have problems...

If you delete a file by accident, you may be able to recover it by using the Undelete utility. For more information on undeleting files, see Chapter 10, "Using PC DOS 7.0 Tools."

Checking the Condition of a Disk

With PC DOS, you can find out how much space is available on a disk, as well as whether the disk is in good condition.

To check a disk, follow these steps:

1. At the PC DOS command prompt, type **CHKDSK**.

2. Press **Enter**. PC DOS checks the disk and displays a status report about the disk's condition and available memory.

The CHKDSK status report displays information in three sections:

■ The first section displays information about the number, size, and condition of files as well as the directories on the disk.

■ The middle section displays information about how much disk space has been allocated, or used, by the files and directories.

■ The third section displays information about system memory.

By using CHKDSK, you quickly can determine the status and condition of your disks. The disk being checked in this report is in good condition.

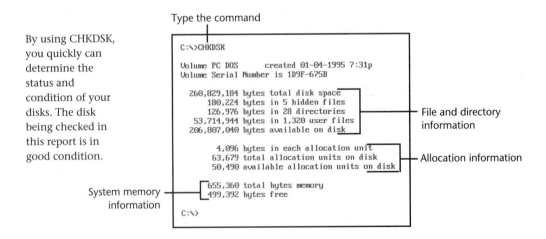

Type the command

```
C:\>CHKDSK

Volume PC DOS      created 01-04-1995 7:31p
Volume Serial Number is 1D9F-675B

   260,829,184 bytes total disk space
       180,224 bytes in 5 hidden files
       126,976 bytes in 28 directories
    53,714,944 bytes in 1,320 user files
   206,807,040 bytes available on disk

         4,096 bytes in each allocation unit
        63,679 total allocation units on disk
        50,490 available allocation units on disk

       655,360 total bytes memory
       499,392 bytes free

C:\>
```

File and directory information

Allocation information

System memory information

When CHKDSK finds allocation errors, a message appears at the top of the status report. You can fix these errors by using the /F switch with the CHKDSK command. Just type **CHKDSK /F** and press **Enter**. Then PC DOS fixes the error.

If CHKDSK finds bad sectors on the disk, you should not use the disk. Bad sectors are areas of the disk where data cannot be written to or read from correctly by the computer. You may be able to copy files from the good sectors on the disk to another disk by using the COPY command. For more information, see the section "Copying a File," earlier in this chapter.

This diskette has bad sectors and should be thrown away.

```
C:\>CHKDSK B:
Volume Serial Number is 3D21-14F6

   1,213,952 bytes total disk space
         512 bytes in 1 hidden files
      24,576 bytes in 2 user files
      15,360 bytes in bad sectors ─────────────── Bad sector information
   1,173,504 bytes available on disk

         512 bytes in each allocation unit
       2,371 total allocation units on disk
       2,292 available allocation units on disk

     655,360 total bytes memory
     499,392 bytes free

C:\>
```

Setting the Date and Time

Personal computers have clocks and calendars that they use to keep track of the time that a file is saved to disk. When you use DIR to list the contents of a directory, you see the date and time on-screen. Some application programs display the time on-screen as you work.

Most computers are set to automatically keep track of the date and time, but some ask you to enter the date and time each time you start the computer. For more information, see the section "Starting PC DOS," earlier in this chapter.

You can change the date and time whenever you want, which is useful for keeping up with daylight savings time or leap year—or when you move your computer across time zones.

To change the date, follow these steps:

1. At the PC DOS command prompt, type **DATE**.

2. Press **Enter**. PC DOS displays the current date and prompts you to enter a new date.

Type the command

You can check the system date or enter a new date by using the DATE command.

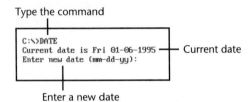

```
C:\>DATE
Current date is Fri 01-06-1995
Enter new date (mm-dd-yy):
```
Current date

Enter a new date

3. Type the date using the format shown within the parentheses on the command line: mm-dd-yy.

4. Press **Enter**. PC DOS changes the date.

If you have problems...   If you already have issued the DATE command but decide that you do not want to change the date, press **Enter** without typing a new date.

If you typed the wrong date, repeat the preceding steps.

To change the time, follow these steps:

1. At the PC DOS command prompt, type **TIME**.

2. Press **Enter**. PC DOS displays the current time and prompts you to enter a new time.

You can check the system time or enter a new time by using the TIME command.

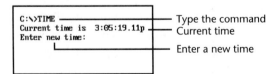

```
C:\>TIME
Current time is  3:05:19.11p
Enter new time:
```
Type the command
Current time

Enter a new time

3. Type the time, using the format that PC DOS uses to display the current time: hh:mm:ssa (for a.m.) or hh:mm:ssp (for p.m.). You do not have to enter seconds.

4. Press **Enter**. PC DOS changes the time.

If you have problems...	If you already have issued the TIME command but decide that you do not want to change the time, press **Enter** without typing a new time.

Setting the Path

PC DOS looks for application programs and commands in the current directory on the current disk. When you want PC DOS to carry out a command or start an application program that is stored somewhere other than in the current directory or disk, you can choose one of three actions:

- You can change directories or disks before you type the command.

- You can type the path to the different location on the command line each time you type a command.

- You can use the PATH command to set PC DOS to look for commands in another directory or disk.

  Note: *You can include the PATH command in your AUTOEXEC.BAT file so that each time you start your computer, PC DOS automatically looks in certain directories for application programs and commands. PATH commands entered at the PC DOS command line take precedence over PATH commands in the AUTOEXEC.BAT file until you reboot your computer. For more information, consult Chapter 8, "Configuring Your Personal Computer."*

To set PC DOS to look for application programs or commands in a different location, follow these steps:

1. Change to the root directory.

2. At the PC DOS command prompt, type the word **PATH**.

3. Press the **spacebar** once.

4. Type the path to the directory where you want PC DOS to look for application programs or commands. The command line should look like the following:

   ```
   C:\>PATH C:\DOS;C:\UTILS;C:\WINDOWS
   ```

The default path for PC DOS is PATH=C:\DOS.

Note: *To add more than one location, separate each directory with a semicolon but no spaces. To add both the DOS directory and the WIN-DOWS directory to the PATH command, type C:\DOS;C:\WINDOWS, for example.*

5. Press **Enter**. PC DOS looks first in the DOS directory, then in the UTILS directory, and then in the WINDOWS directory.

Checking the System Memory

You need to know how much memory is available on your computer. Most application programs have minimum memory requirements, and you should make sure that your computer meets those requirements before you try to use the programs.

To find out how much memory is available on your computer and how the memory is allocated, follow these steps:

1. At the PC DOS command prompt, type **MEM**.

2. Press **Enter**. PC DOS displays a status report detailing your system memory.

Type the command

By using the MEM command, you can see how much memory you have on your system, how the memory is allocated, and how much memory is available.

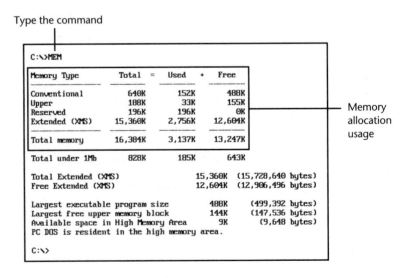

Memory allocation usage

The MEM command displays information about different types of memory—conventional, upper, adapter RAM/ROM, extended, and expanded or reserved. (To learn more about memory and about optimizing the allocation of memory on your computer, see Chapter 8, "Configuring Your Personal Computer.")

2

Chapter 3

Working with the Windows Desktop

Graphical user interface
An easy-to-use method of combining graphics, menus, and plain English commands so that the user can communicate with the computer.

Microsoft Windows is a powerful operating environment that enables you to access the power of PC DOS without memorizing PC DOS commands and syntax. Windows uses a *graphical user interface* (GUI) so that you easily can see on-screen the tools you need to complete specific file- and program-management tasks.

Windows provides many useful tools and accessories for managing your data and running your application programs. This chapter, an overview of the Windows environment, is designed to help you learn the basics of Windows, including starting Windows, identifying the different parts of the Windows desktop, and using the mouse to navigate throughout the desktop.

After you understand the basics of the Windows environment, you can move on to later chapters, which provide more detail on using Windows to accomplish specific tasks.

Note: *Some versions of Windows may look different from the version used to illustrate this book. The functions, however, work the same way.*

Starting Windows

To start Windows from the PC DOS command prompt, follow these steps:

    1. Type **WIN**.

2. Press **Enter**. Windows begins loading. When it is loaded, you see the Program Manager window open on-screen.

The first time you start Windows, the PC DOS 7.0 Tools program group window usually is open on the desktop.

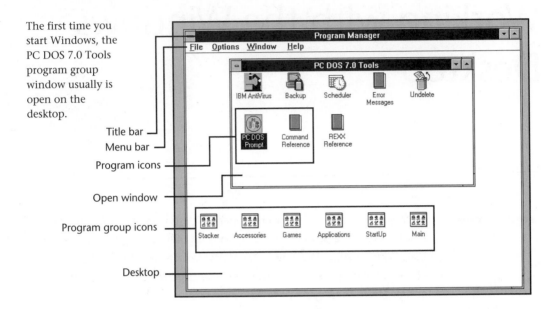

Title bar

Menu bar

Program icons

Open window

Program group icons

Desktop

Window

A rectangular area on-screen in which you view program icons, application programs, or documents.

The Program Manager *window* includes many different elements, such as the menu bar, title bar, and icons. Your Program Manager window may look different from the window used in this book's illustrations. You may have different program group icons across the bottom of the Program Manager window, for example.

Using a Mouse in Windows

Mouse

A pointing device used in many application programs to make choices, select data, and otherwise communicate with the computer.

Windows is designed for use with a *mouse*. Although you can get by with just a keyboard, using a mouse is much easier. This book assumes that you are using a mouse. If you are using a keyboard, consult your Windows User's Guide for more information.

In the Windows desktop, you can use a mouse to perform the following tasks:

- Opening windows
- Closing windows
- Opening menus

■ Choosing menu commands

■ Rearranging on-screen items, such as icons and windows

Note: *For more information about performing specific tasks in Windows, see Chapter 4, "Making Windows Work."*

The position of the mouse is indicated on-screen by a mouse pointer. Usually, the mouse pointer is an arrow, but it sometimes changes shape depending on the current action.

Mouse pad
A pad that provides a uniform surface for a mouse to slide on.

The mouse pointer moves on-screen according to the movements of the mouse on your desk or on a *mouse pad*. To move the mouse pointer, simply move the mouse.

3

The three basic mouse actions follow:

■ *Click.* To point to an item and quickly press and release the left mouse button. You click to select an item, such as an option on a menu. To cancel a selection, click an empty area of the desktop.

■ *Double-click.* To point to an item and then press and release the left mouse button twice, as quickly as possible. You double-click to open or close windows and to start applications from icons.

■ *Drag.* To point to an item, press and hold the left mouse button as you move the pointer to another location, and then release the mouse button. You drag to resize windows, move icons, and scroll.

Note: *Unless otherwise specified, you use the left mouse button for all mouse actions.*

If you have problems...

If you try to double-click but nothing happens, you may not be clicking fast enough. Try again.

Understanding the Windows Desktop

Desktop
The background of the screen, on which windows, icons, and dialog boxes appear.

Your screen provides a background for Windows, called a *desktop*. On the desktop, each application is displayed in its own window (hence the name Windows). All windows have the same set of controls that enable you to move, resize, and manipulate the window.

If you have multiple windows open, they may overlap on the desktop, just as papers on your desk can be stacked one on top of the other. The first time you start Windows, the PC DOS 7.0 Tools program group window usually is open on top of the Program Manager window.

To use Microsoft Windows effectively, you should learn the different parts of the Windows desktop.

The Title Bar

Across the top of each window is its title bar. At the right side of the title bar are the Minimize button for reducing windows to icons and the Maximize button for expanding windows to fill the desktop. At the left side of the title bar is the Control menu icon, a box with a small hyphen in it. The Control icon activates a window's Control menu.

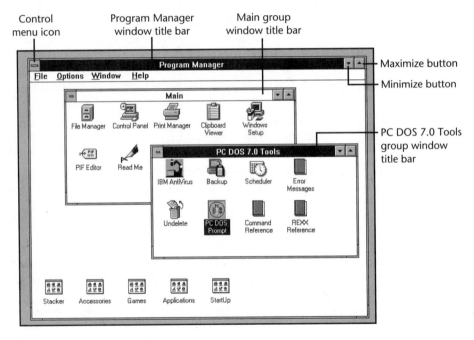

Control menu icon

Program Manager window title bar

Main group window title bar

Every open window has a title bar, used to identify the contents of the window.

Maximize button

Minimize button

PC DOS 7.0 Tools group window title bar

Menus

Menus enable you to select options to perform functions or carry out commands. The Control menu enables you to control the size and position of its window, for example. Some windows have a menu bar below the title bar. When you select an item from the menu bar, a menu drops down into the window.

Choose a menu
command here

Menus, like the
Control menu
shown here,
enable you to
choose commands
without remem-
bering syntax,
switches, or
parameters.

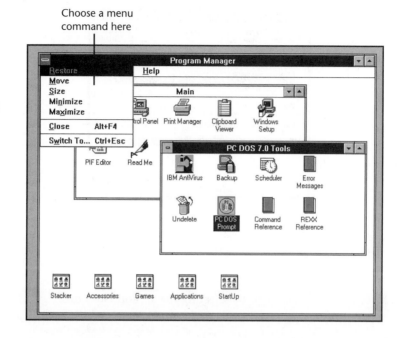

3

Dialog Boxes

Some menu options require that you enter additional information. When
you select one of these options, a dialog box opens. You type the additional information into a text box, select from a list of options, or select a
button.

In a dialog box,
you provide
additional
information that
Windows needs to
complete the
command.

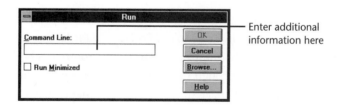

Enter additional
information here

Buttons

Buttons are on-screen areas with which you select actions or commands.
Most dialog boxes have at least a Cancel button, which stops the current
activity and returns to the preceding screen; an OK button, which ac-
cepts the current activity; and a Help button, which opens a Help window. Some windows have buttons, too. You can use the Minimize and
Maximize buttons to control the size of the current window.

By using buttons,
you can set
options or choose
commands.

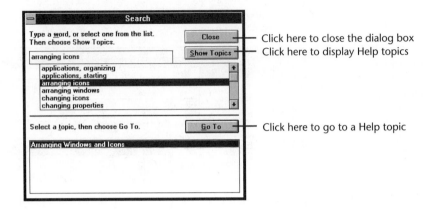

Icons

Icons are small pictures used to identify groups of application programs, files, or directories. You open windows, start application programs, and select items by selecting the appropriate icons.

Understanding the Program Manager

The Program Manager is the central Microsoft Windows program. When you start Microsoft Windows, the Program Manager starts automatically. When you exit Microsoft Windows, you exit the Program Manager. You cannot run Microsoft Windows if you are not running the Program Manager.

The Program Manager does what its name implies—it manages application programs. You use the Program Manager to organize application programs into groups called program groups, establishing a set that can be accessed through the same program group window. Usually, programs in a group are related, either by functionality (such as a group of accessories) or by usage (such as a group of application programs used to compile a monthly newsletter).

Each program group is represented by a program group icon.

After you double-
click a program
group icon, a
group window
opens.

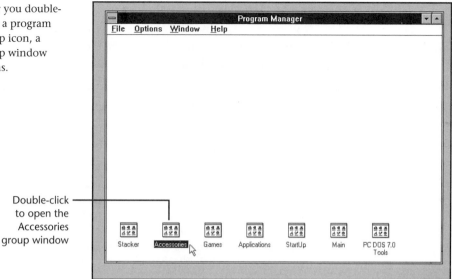

Double-click
to open the
Accessories
group window

In each program group window, you see the icons for each program item
in the group.

After you double-
click a program
icon, the program
starts.

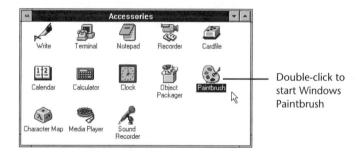

Double-click to
start Windows
Paintbrush

Windows sets up some program groups automatically. You see their icons
at the bottom of the Program Manager screen:

■ *Main program group.* Within this group, you find Microsoft
Windows system application programs, which are programs that
help you work with your system (computer). The Main program
group includes the File Manager, Print Manager, DOS Prompt, Windows Setup, Control Panel, Clipboard, and other application program items.

■ *Accessories program group*. This group contains accessory programs that are provided with Microsoft Windows. The following list includes some of these programs.

Program	Function
Calculator	Displays a calculator.
Clock	Displays the time.
Notepad	Enables you to enter, print, and edit notes.
Calendar	Enables you to enter and review appointments.
Cardfile	Enables you to enter, edit, sort, and delete cards in card file.
Write	Enables you to create, edit, format, and print word processing documents.
Paintbrush	Enables you to create, edit, and print drawings. Paintbrush is a complete drawing program.

Note: *For information about starting application programs and about using the Windows accessories, see Chapter 4, "Making Windows Work."*

■ *Games program group*. The Games program group contains two games: Solitaire and Minesweeper.

■ *StartUp group*. This group is empty until you add application programs to it. Applications you place in the StartUp group start when you enter Windows.

■ *Applications group*. When you install Microsoft Windows, the Setup program looks at the application programs on your hard disk. If you have any application programs that Microsoft Windows recognizes, Setup creates program icons for them and stores them in a group named Windows Applications. Setup also creates a group for Non-Windows Applications.

Exiting Windows

You always should exit Windows before turning off your computer. To exit Windows and return to the PC DOS command prompt, follow these steps:

1. Close all open windows and applications.

2. Point to **F**ile in the menu bar, and click the left mouse button.

3. Point to E**x**it Windows, and click the left mouse button. Windows prompts you to confirm that you want to exit.

4. Point to OK, and click the left mouse button. Windows closes, and the PC DOS command prompt is displayed.

Tip

As a shortcut to exit Windows, double-click the Control menu button at the far left of the Program Manager title bar. Windows prompts you to confirm that you want to exit. Click OK.

3

Chapter 4

Making Windows Work

Application program
A computer program designed to help you perform tasks, such as writing a report— also called an application.

One of the primary benefits of Windows is that all Windows *application programs* use similar operating concepts. After you learn to use one Windows application program, you can use them all.

From the Windows desktop, you have access to the menus, icons, windows, and dialog boxes you need to manage programs and files. In this chapter, you learn to use the Program Manager to organize the desktop. You learn to control the size and position of windows and icons, to organize application programs into groups, and to start applications. You even learn to use the PC DOS command prompt without turning off Windows. To make sure that you don't get stuck along the way, this chapter first presents how to display Help information for all Windows tasks.

Getting Help

Almost every Windows application program has a Help menu. From the Help menu, you can start a Help program to display information about many aspects of the application program.

To display Help information, take one of the following actions:

Context-sensitive
Pertaining to the current action.

- Press **F1**. The Help program starts, and a *context-sensitive* Help window opens.

- Choose **H**elp from the menu bar, and choose one of the Help menu commands.

If you have problems...	To choose a menu item, point to it with the mouse, and then click the left mouse button.

Displaying Help for a Topic

To display Help for a particular topic, follow these steps:

1. Choose **H**elp from the menu bar.

2. Choose **C**ontents from the Help menu. A Help Window opens; it displays the main topics for which Help is available.

The Help window groups topics into How To and Commands categories.

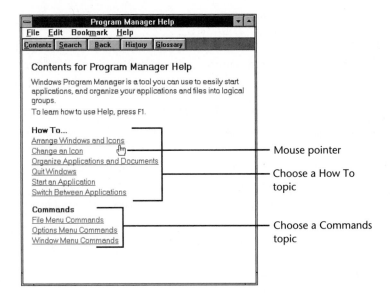

3. Choose the topic for which you want additional information. Windows displays the Help information.

Note: *In the Help program, when the mouse pointer is on a topic for which you can get help, the pointer changes to a hand with a pointing finger.*

Closing the Help Window

To close the Help window, take one of the following actions:

■ Choose **C**lose from the Help window's Control menu.

■ Choose E**x**it from the Help window's **F**ile menu.

■ Double-click the Control menu button.

Control menu button

— Click to display the Help table of contents

— Choose to search for a Help topic

Most Windows
application
programs have
similar Help
programs. This
screen displays
Help for using the
Program Manager.
To scroll through
the Help screen,
click one of the
scroll arrows on
the right side of
the screen.

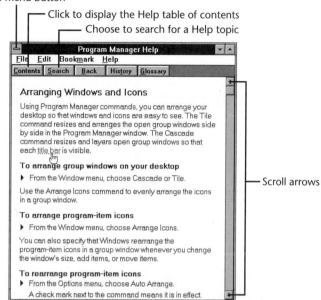

Scroll arrows

If you have problems... To open the Control menu, click the Control menu button at the far left end of the window's title bar.

Getting Comfortable with Windows

To be comfortable using Windows, you need to know how to control your Windows desktop. Controlling the desktop means, in large part, controlling the windows themselves.

All the windows that appear in Windows, including the Program Manager, can be opened, closed, moved, and resized. In this section, you learn the basic tasks involved in manipulating windows so that you easily can access the information you need.

Opening a Window

To open a window, double-click the appropriate icon.

When you double-click a program group icon, you open a group window. When you double-click a program icon, you start that program. For more information on starting programs, see the section "Starting Application Programs Automatically," later in this chapter.

If you have problems...   If a Control menu opens instead of a window, you are not double-clicking fast enough. Try again, or choose **R**estore from the Control menu.

You can continue opening windows until the desktop is full or until the computer runs out of memory.

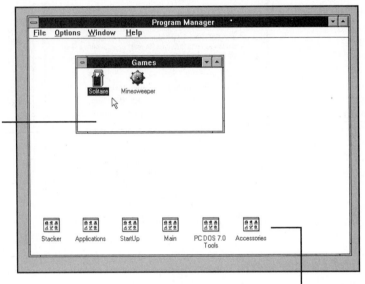

The Games group window is open and active

Double-click to open the Accessories group window

Don't worry if your screen looks different from the screens used to illustrate this book. Your desktop may be organized differently. You still can perform all the same tasks.

Note: *You also can use the Control menu to open a window. Click the icon to display the Control menu. Then click **R**estore.*

Changing the Active Window

Active window
The window in which you currently are working.

No matter how many windows are open on the desktop, you can work in only the *active window*.

You can tell which window is active in two ways:

- The active window is on top of other open windows on the desktop.

- The title bar of the active window is highlighted.

Four windows are
open. The PC DOS
7.0 Tools group
window is the
active window.

Title bar of the
active window
is highlighted

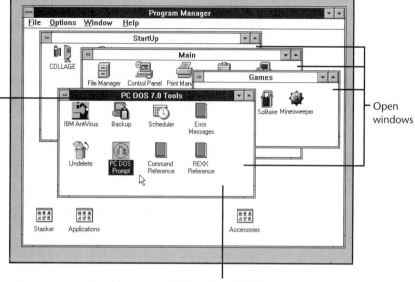

Open
windows

Active window is on top

To make a window active, click anywhere in it. The window moves to the top of the stack of windows, and its title bar appears in a different color or shade.

If you have problems...

If the window you want to make active is hidden behind another window, click **W**indow on the menu bar to open the Window menu. From the list of available windows, choose the one you want to make active.

Resizing a Window

You can change the size of any open window by dragging its borders with the mouse.

To resize a window, follow these steps:

1. Point to the border you want to move.

Note: *When you are pointing to the border, the mouse pointer changes shape to a double-headed arrow.*

4

2. Press and hold down the left mouse button, and drag the border to its new location. As you drag, you see the border move along with the mouse pointer.

3. Release the mouse button. The window adjusts to the new size.

New position
of border

To resize a
window, drag one
of its borders.

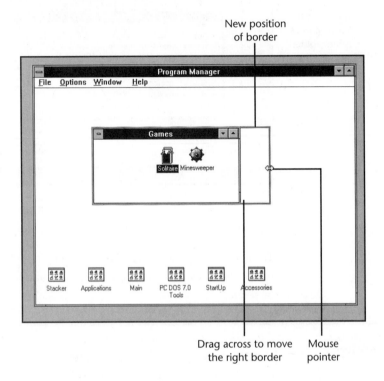

Drag across to move   Mouse
the right border   pointer

Note: *To change the height and width of the window simultaneously, drag one of the window's corners.*

If you have problems...   If nothing happens when you try to change a window's size, you probably are not pointing at a border. Make sure that the mouse pointer changes to a double-headed arrow before you drag the border.

Note: *You also can resize a window by choosing Size from its Control menu and using the arrow keys to move the borders. Press **Enter** when the window is the size you want.*

Moving a Window

You can move a window to a different location on-screen by dragging it with the mouse.

To move a window, follow these steps:

1. Point to the window's title bar.

2. Press and hold down the left mouse button, and drag the window to the new location. You see the borders of the window move with the mouse pointer.

3. Release the mouse button.

You can move a
window to any
location on the
desktop.

Mouse pointer ——

Drag the title bar ——
to move the window

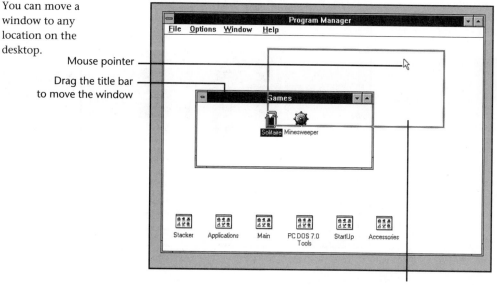

New window position

**If you have
problems...** If nothing happens when you try to move a window, you probably are not pointing to the window's title bar. Make sure that the mouse pointer is within the title bar before you drag the window.

Note: *You also can move a window by choosing* **M***ove from the window's Control menu and then using the arrow keys on the numeric keypad to move the window. Press* **Enter** *when the window is positioned as you want it.*

Maximizing a Window

Maximize
To increase the size of a window until it covers the desktop.

You can *maximize* a window to fill the entire desktop. Maximizing a window gives you more room to work.

To maximize a window, perform one of the following actions:

- Click the Maximize button at the far right of the window's title bar. This button has an arrowhead pointing up.

- Choose **M**aximize from the window's Control menu.

Click to maximize the Program Manager window

Each window has a Maximize button at the right end of its title bar.

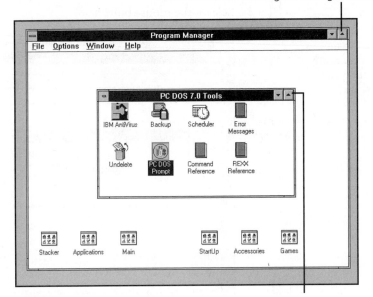

Click to maximize the PC DOS 7.0 Tools window

Minimizing a Window

Minimize
To reduce a window to an icon.

You can *minimize* a window that you are not currently using.

To minimize a window, take one of the following actions:

- Click the Minimize button on the title bar. This button has an arrowhead pointing down.

- Choose Mi**n**imize from the window's Control menu.

Minimize buttons

Each window has a
Minimize button,
which you can use
to minimize the
window to an
icon.

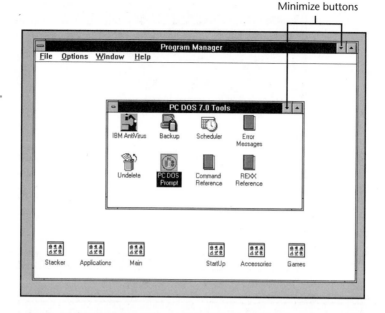

Note: *Program group windows, such as the Main group, are reduced to pro-gram group icons at the bottom of the Program Manager. Application program, utility, or document icons are positioned at the bottom of the desktop, behind any active windows. The application program that has been minimized still is active; it is just out of the way.*

Restoring a Window

Restore

To return a window
to its most recent
size and position
on the desktop.

You can *restore* a window that has been maximized or minimized to its most recent size and location.

To restore a window to its previous size, take one of the following actions:

■ Click the Restore button, which replaces the Maximize button on the title bar. The Restore button has arrowheads pointing up and down.

■ Choose **R**estore from the window's Control menu.

Here, the PC DOS 7.0 Tools window is maximized. When you maximize a window, the Restore button appears at the right end of the title bar below the Maximize button.

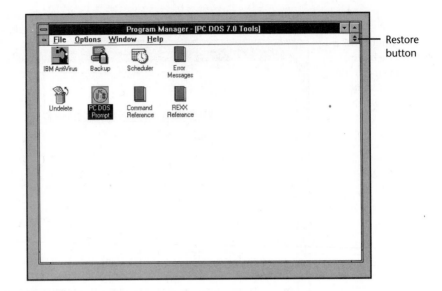

Restore button

If you have problems...

If you try to restore the window but nothing happens, the window has not been maximized or minimized. You cannot restore a window unless it first has been maximized or minimized.

Arranging the Windows on Your Desktop

Tile
To arrange open windows on the desktop so they do not overlap.

Cascade
To arrange open windows on the desktop so they overlap, while a portion of each window is visible.

Sometimes a desktop becomes so cluttered with open windows that you cannot tell what you are using. When that happens, you can choose to *tile* or to *cascade* the open windows on-screen so that you can see them all.

To arrange the windows on the desktop, follow these steps:

1. Choose **W**indow from the menu bar to drop down the Window menu.

2. Choose one of the following options:

   ■ **T**ile arranges the windows on-screen so that no window is overlapping another.

   ■ **C**ascade arranges the windows on-screen so that they overlap.

The windows
are tiled on
the desktop.

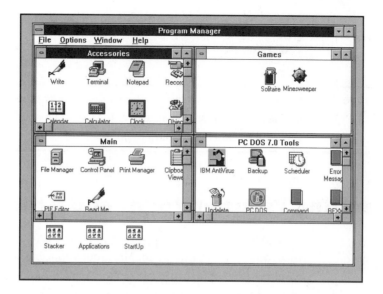

The windows are
cascaded on the
desktop.

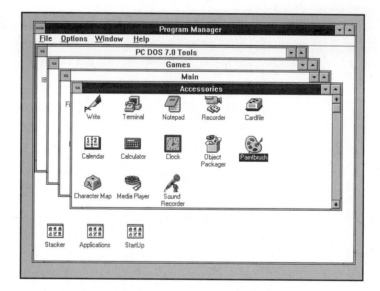

Closing a Window

To close a window, perform one of the following actions:

■ Choose **C**lose from the window's Control menu. (To open the
   Control menu, click the Control menu button at the far left end
   of the window's title bar.)

■ Choose **C**lose from the window's **F**ile menu.

■ Double-click the Control menu button.

If you have problems... If the Exit Windows dialog box appears, you clicked the Control menu box for the Program Manager instead of the Control menu box for the window you want to close. Click Cancel.

Organizing Program Items and Groups

With Windows, you can organize application programs into groups so that you easily can find them. The groups appear on-screen in Group windows, from which you can launch application programs and complete other program- and file-management tasks.

When you install Windows, several program groups are created automatically. Most people have a Main program group and an Accessories program group that Windows created, for example.

You can group application programs in many different combinations, and you easily can add, delete, or move them from groups. You even can place application programs in more than one group without keeping more than one copy of the program on disk.

Changing a Program Group Name

Below every program group icon is the program group's name. When you open the program group window, the name appears in the title bar. You can change a program group name at any time.

To change a program group name, follow these steps:

1. Click the program group icon to select it. The program group's Control menu appears.

2. Click **F**ile in the Program Manager menu bar to open the File menu. Don't worry that the Control menu disappears. You do not need it now.

3. Choose **P**roperties from the File menu. The Program Group Properties dialog box appears. Inside this box, you see two text boxes: **D**escription and **G**roup File. The **D**escription text box contains the current program group name. (The mouse pointer is positioned inside this box.)

In the Program Group Properties dialog box, you can change the name of the selected program group.

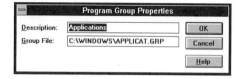

4. In the **D**escription text box, type the new program group name.

5. Choose OK, or press **Enter**. You see the new name below the program group icon.

Adding a New Program Group

Windows creates some program groups during setup. You can add a new program group at any time.

To add a new program group, follow these steps:

1. Close all program group windows.

2. Choose **F**ile from the menu bar to open the File menu.

3. Choose **N**ew from the File menu. You see the New Program Object dialog box. The Program **G**roup option is selected.

In the New Program Object dialog box, you choose to add a new program group.

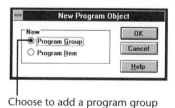

Choose to add a program group

If you have problems...

If Program **I**tem is selected instead of Program **G**roup, you did not close all program group windows before choosing **F**ile, **N**ew. Windows assumes that you want to add a program item to the active group window. Choose Cancel. Close all windows, and then try again.

---

4. Click OK. You see the Program Group Properties dialog box. Inside this box, you see two text boxes: **D**escription and **G**roup File.

5. In the **D**escription text box, type a name for the new program group.

Type the new program group name

In the Program Group Properties dialog box, you enter a name for the new program group.

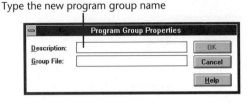

6. Click OK. Windows opens the new program group window. (Windows inserts the path into the Group File text box.)

The new program group contains no program icons yet, but the program group name appears in the window's title bar.

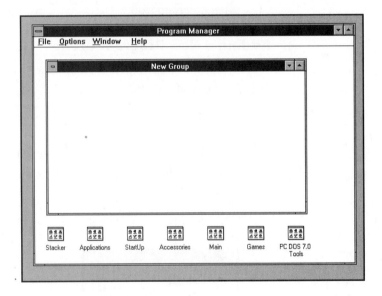

Moving a Program to a Different Group

To move program items from one group to another, follow these steps:

1. Open the group window that contains the item you want to move.

2. Open the group window to which you want to move the item.

3. Arrange the windows so that you can see both windows on-screen.

Note: *You can arrange the windows by resizing and moving them or by tiling them on the desktop.*

4. Point to the icon for the item you want to move.

5. Press and hold down the mouse button, and drag the icon to the other window.

6. Release the mouse button.

You easily can drag an icon from one window to another.

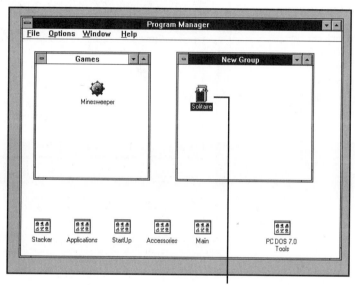

The moved icon

Copying a Program Item to Another Group

You can place a program item in more than one group.

To copy a program item from one group into another group, follow these steps:

1. Open the program group window that contains the program item you want to copy.

2. Open the program group window to which you want to copy the program item.

3. Arrange the windows so that you can see them both on-screen.

4. Point to the icon you want to copy.

5. Press and hold down **Ctrl**.

6. Press and hold down the mouse button.

7. While continuing to hold down both **Ctrl** and the mouse button, drag the icon to the other program group window.

8. Release the mouse button and **Ctrl**.

The copied icon appears in the new group and the original group. The program it represents now is part of both program groups.

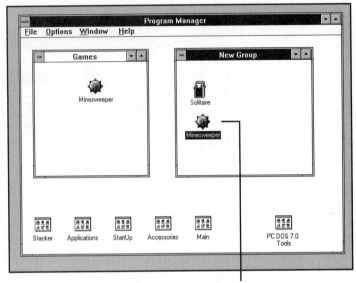

The copied icon

Deleting a Program Icon

To delete a program icon and remove the application program from that group, follow these steps:

1. Open the group window that contains the program icon you want to delete.

2. Click the icon you want to delete.

3. Choose **F**ile, **D**elete. The Delete dialog box appears.

4. Choose **Y**es to confirm that you want to delete the selected icon.

Windows prompts you for confirmation before deleting an icon.

> ### Tip
>
> To quickly remove an application program from a group, drag the icon out of the group window and onto the desktop. When you see a No symbol (a circle with a slash through it), release the mouse button. The icon disappears.

Note: *When you delete a program item icon, you don't delete the program files on disk. The files still are there, but the item no longer is part of the program group.*

You can delete a program group icon by using the same methods you use to delete a program item icon. When you delete a program group icon, all item icons in that group also are deleted.

Adding a New Program Icon

To add a new program item to a program group, follow these steps:

1. Open the program group window to which you want to add a new program item.

2. Choose **F**ile, **N**ew. The New Program Object dialog box appears. The Program **I**tem option is selected.

In the New Program Object dialog box, choose to create a new program item.

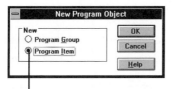

Choose to create a new program item

3. Click OK. You see the Program Item Properties dialog box. Inside this box, you see these text boxes: **D**escription, **C**ommand Line, **W**orking Directory, and **S**hortcut Key.

In the Program
Item Properties
dialog box, you
specify a name
and start-up
options for the
new program
item.

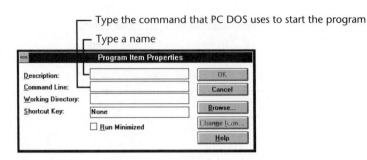

Type the command that PC DOS uses to start the program

Type a name

Program Item Properties

Description:

Command Line:

Working Directory:

Shortcut Key: None

☐ Run Minimized

OK

Cancel

Browse...

Change Icon...

Help

4. In the **D**escription text box, type the name you want to appear below the icon in the program group window.

   This step enters a name for the new application program and moves the insertion point to the **C**ommand Line text box.

5. In the **C**ommand Line text box, type the command that starts the application program from the PC DOS command prompt. If necessary, include the complete path to the application program, including the name of the directory containing the application program. (For information about the command used to start the application program, consult its documentation. For information about paths, see Chapter 1, "Understanding System Basics.")

6. Choose OK.

Tip

To move from one text box to another, click the mouse pointer in the text box, or press Tab.

Note: *Adding an application program isn't always easy. You have to know the command name and where that file is kept on your hard disk.*

Arranging Icons within a Window

You can move and rearrange icons on the desktop. To move an icon, follow these steps:

1. Point to the icon you want to move.

2. Press and hold down the left mouse button.

3. Drag the icon to the new location.

To arrange all icons neatly within a window, follow these steps:

1. Make the window that contains the icons the active window.

2. Choose **W**indow from the menu bar to drop down the Window menu.

3. Choose **A**rrange Icons.

Changing an Application Program's Icon

Windows comes with a selection of icons and usually automatically assigns icons to new program items and program groups. You can select a different icon at any time, however.

To change an application program's icon, follow these steps:

1. Open the program group that contains the icon you want to change.

2. Choose the icon you want to change.

3. Choose **F**ile, **P**roperties. You see the Program Item Properties dialog box.

In the Program Item Properties dialog box, you can see the current program item icon and choose a different icon.

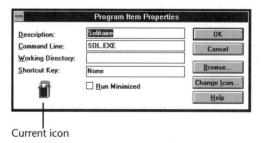

Current icon

4. In the Program Item Properties dialog box, click the Change **I**con button. The Change Icon dialog box appears.

5. In the Change Icon dialog box, click the **B**rowse button. The Browse dialog box appears.

6. In the Browse dialog box, scroll through the File **N**ame list until you see the file MORICONS.DLL.

In the Browse
dialog box, you
can select any file
that contains
additional icons.

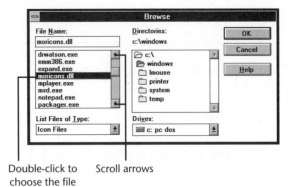

Double-click to   Scroll arrows
choose the file

7. Double-click the MORICONS file to select it. The icons are
displayed in the Change Icon dialog box.

8. In the **C**urrent Icon box, choose the icon you want to use.

Use the scroll
arrows below the
Current Icon box
to scroll through
the list of icons.

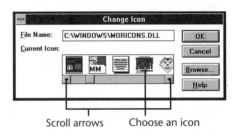

Scroll arrows   Choose an icon

9. Choose OK to return to the Program Item Properties dialog box.

10. Choose OK to assign the new icon to the program item.

Running Application Programs in Windows

In Windows, application programs run within application windows. To
run an application program, you open its window. You can have more
than one window open at a time, although you can work only in the
active window.

Windows provides many different ways to open application windows. In
this section, you learn to start application programs and to switch among
them.

Starting an Application Program by Using Its Icon

The fastest way to start an application program in Windows is to use its program item icon.

To start an application program from a program item icon, follow these steps:

1. Open the program group window that contains the application program you want to start.

2. Double-click the program item icon. A small hourglass indicates that Windows is starting the application program.

Double-click to start IBM AntiVirus

Double-click to start the Scheduler

You quickly can start an application program by double-clicking its program item icon.

PC DOS 7.0 Tools

IBM AntiVirus   Backup   Scheduler   Error Messages

Undelete   PC DOS Prompt   Command Reference   REXX Reference

If you have problems...

If the application program doesn't start, you probably did not click twice. Point to the icon again, and press and release the mouse button twice in rapid succession.

Running an Application Program from the File Menu

You can use the File menu to run any application program, even if it has not been added to a program group. You can run application programs from diskettes or from the hard disk.

To start an application program by using the File menu, follow these steps:

1. Choose **F**ile, **R**un. The Run dialog box appears.

You can run any
program by typing
its command line
in the Run dialog
box.

2. In the **C**ommand Line text box, type the command you use to start
   the application program from the PC DOS command prompt. If
   necessary, enter the full path to the program files.

3. Click OK. Windows starts loading the application program.

**If you have
problems...**

If the application program doesn't start, you probably did not type the
correct command line. Check your spelling, and make sure that you
have entered the full path to the program files. Consult the application
program's documentation for more information on the correct command.

Running More Than One Application Program

One of the benefits of Windows is that you can run application programs
simultaneously. Each application program runs in its own window; you
can switch back and forth among the open application programs and
even copy information from one application program to another.

To start more than one application program, follow these steps:

1. Start the first application program, using any of the methods
   described in the previous sections.

2. Take one of the following actions to return to the Program
   Manager:

   - Press **Alt+Tab**.

   - Press **Ctrl+Esc** to display the Task List. Choose Program
     Manager, and then choose **S**witch To.

   - Click within the Program Manager window if you can see it
     on-screen.

3. Open another application program, using any of the methods
   described in the previous sections.

To return to the
Program Manager
to start another
application
program, click
within the
Program Manager
window.

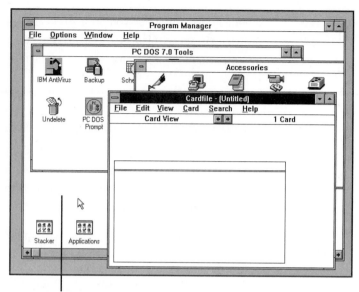

Click to make the Program Manager window active

Switching among Open Application Programs

You can switch among open application programs by taking any of the
following actions:

- If you can see the application program window on-screen, click in
  it. It becomes the active window.

- Press **Ctrl+Esc** to display the Task List. Choose the application
  program you want to make active, and then choose **S**witch To.

Use the Task List
to change among
open application
programs.

- Press and hold down the **Alt** key, and then press the **Tab** key
  to display the name and icon of the next open application
  program. Continue holding down **Alt** and pressing **Tab** until
  the application program you want to make active is displayed;
  release **Alt** and **Tab**.

If you have problems...

If nothing happens when you press **Alt+Tab**, Application Fast Alt+Tab Switching is not enabled. See your Windows documentation for more information. In the meantime, try one of the other methods described in this section.

Starting Application Programs Automatically

If you want an application program to start automatically whenever you start Windows, you can add that application program to the StartUp program group. Windows starts all programs in the StartUp program group each time you start Windows.

To add application programs to the StartUp program group, follow these steps:

1. Open the group window that contains the program item you want to start automatically.

2. Open the StartUp program group window.

Windows automatically starts all programs in the StartUp program group each time Windows starts.

3. Arrange the windows so that you can see them both on-screen.

4. Copy the icon for the application program you want to start automatically to the StartUp program group window. For more information, see the section "Copying a Program Item to Another Group," earlier in this chapter.

Exiting an Application Program

Most Windows application programs use the same exit procedures. For specific information about a particular application program, consult its documentation.

To exit a Windows application program, take one of the following actions:

- Double-click the application program window's Control menu button.

- Choose **F**ile, E**x**it.

- Press **Alt+F4**.

Usually, the program prompts you to save any changes you have made.

Note: *Be sure to exit all application programs before exiting Windows.*

Using Windows Accessories

Windows accessories are programs that can augment and enhance your Windows application programs. You can leave accessories open or minimized while you use other application programs so that you can access them quickly and easily. You can maximize any accessory window to give yourself more room to work.

During setup, Windows places the accessories programs in a program group called Accessories.

To see the icons for the accessories, open the Accessories group window.

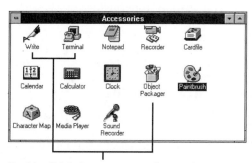

Double-click its icon to start an Accessories program

Accessories perform different functions, but they operate in a manner similar to the operation of other Windows application programs.

Starting and Using an Accessory

To start most accessories, open the Accessories group window, and double-click the accessory icon.

To open a new file in an accessory, choose **N**ew from the File menu. A new, untitled file opens.

To open an existing file in an accessory program, follow these steps:

1. Choose **F**ile, **O**pen. The Open dialog box appears.

2. In the Open dialog box, select the name of the file you want to open. If necessary, select the drive and directory first. Most accessories are associated with a specific file extension, but you can display and select files with different extensions by using the List Files of **T**ype drop-down list.

3. Choose OK.

Note: *You can open only one file at a time in Windows accessories. When you open a new file, the file you were working in closes. To open another file in the same accessory, go back to the Program Manager and double-click the icon.*

Saving an Accessory File

To save a file while in an accessory, follow these steps:

1. Choose **F**ile, **S**ave. If you are saving a file for the first time, the Save As dialog box appears.

2. Enter the file name. If necessary, enter the drive and directory where you want to store the file.

3. Choose OK.

Note: *To save an accessory file with a new name, choose File, Save As.*

Printing an Accessory File

To print a file in an accessory, follow these steps:

1. Choose P**r**int Setup to select a printer and to set printer options.

2. Choose **F**ile, **P**rint.

Closing an Accessory

To exit an accessory, take one of the following actions:

- Choose **F**ile, E**x**it.

- Double-click the Control menu button on the title bar.

- Choose **C**lose from the Control menu.

If you have not saved changes to the current file, a dialog box prompts you to save your changes before closing.

Exploring the Accessories

Most Windows accessories come standard with Windows. Some, however, are available only if your system can use them. Chat, WinMeter, and Net Watcher, for example, are present only on networked systems. Media Player and Sound Recorder can be used only on multimedia computers. Descriptions of some of the accessories follow.

Windows Write

Write is a word processing accessory designed specifically for Windows. This accessory uses the Windows environment to simplify basic editing, formatting, and text-management tasks. Write also enables you to link text with data from other Windows application programs.

To start Write, select the Write icon from the Program Manager Accessories group window.

The Write window opens with a new, untitled document file displayed.

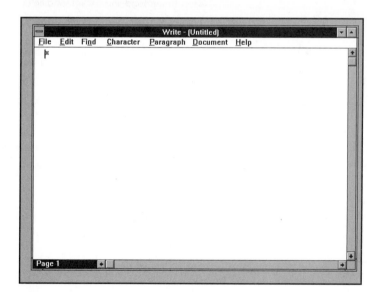

Windows Paintbrush

Paintbrush is a graphics accessory that enables you to create pictures that can be used by themselves or incorporated into other Windows application programs.

To start Paintbrush, select the Paintbrush icon from the Program
Manager Accessories group window.

The Paintbrush
window opens
with a new,
untitled file
displayed.

Select a tool

Select a line width

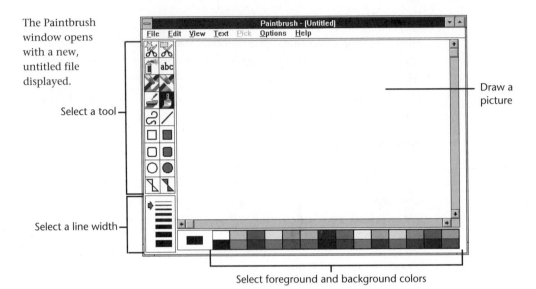

Draw a
picture

Select foreground and background colors

Notepad

The Notepad is a limited text editor, which you can use to open, edit,
and save text files. Notepad cannot hold graphics files. You can use the
Notepad to jot notes and to store text you want to move from one application program to another.

To start the Notepad, choose the Notepad icon in the Accessories group
window.

The Notepad window opens with a new, untitled file displayed.

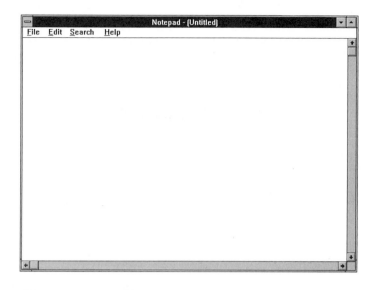

Cardfile

The Cardfile stores files containing stacks of index cards. You can copy or print information from a card. You can use the cards to dial phone numbers on a modem or to start application programs from embedded objects.

To start the Cardfile, choose the Cardfile icon in the Accessories group window.

In Cardfile, enter card information below the double line. Enter the title or index information above the double line.

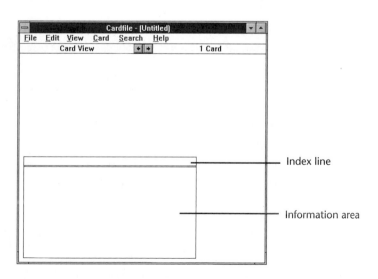

Index line

Information area

Calendar

Use the Calendar to set appointments, mark special days, and issue an alarm. To open the Calendar, choose the Calendar icon from the Accessories group window.

When you open the Calendar, the daily view is displayed, marked in hourly intervals. Choose **M**onth from the **V**iew menu to display the monthly view.

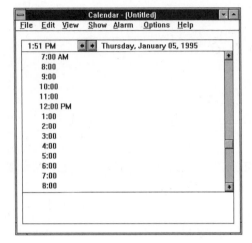

Calculator

Use the Calculator to perform mathematical and scientific calculations. With the mouse, click the keys in the Calculator window. With a keyboard, press the corresponding key on the keyboard. Special function keys follow:

Keyboard Functions

Keys	Function	Calculator Key
Ctrl+L	Clear memory	MC
Ctrl+R	Display memory	MR
Ctrl+P	Add to memory	M+
Ctrl+M	Store value in memory	MS
Del	Delete displayed value	CE
Backspace	Delete last digit in displayed value	Back
F9	Change sign	+/-
@	Square root	sqrt
R	Calculate reciprocal	1/x
Esc	Clear	C

Use the Calculator to perform mathematical functions while you work.

Clock

Open the Clock to check the time. Use the Settings menu to change the appearance of the clock. To set the time, use the Date/Time item in the Windows Control Panel.

Minimize the Clock window to keep it displayed on the desktop while you work.

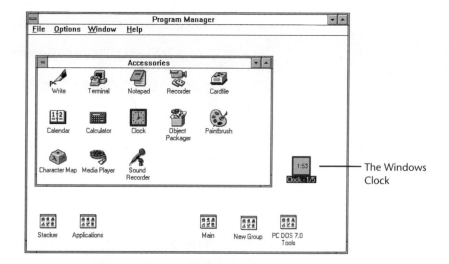

The Windows Clock

Using the Windows Clipboard

Another Windows feature worth mentioning is the Clipboard. The Clipboard is a temporary storage area that you can use to copy selected text or objects among any Windows accessory or application program files. You must use the Clipboard from within any Windows application program—it does not run in its own window.

To copy selected text or objects from any file to the Clipboard, select the item in the file. Then choose **E**dit, **C**opy.

To copy text or objects from the Clipboard into a file, open the file and position the cursor where you want the item placed. Then choose **E**dit, **P**aste.

To view and save the item currently stored in the Clipboard, use the Clipboard Viewer. To open the Clipboard Viewer, double-click the Clipboard Viewer icon from the Main group window, not from the Accessories group window.

The Clipboard is a useful feature in Windows. You also can use it to link and embed objects from one application program to another.

Accessing the PC DOS Command Prompt

You can access the PC DOS command prompt without closing Windows. To access the PC DOS command prompt, follow these steps:

1. Open the PC DOS 7.0 Tools program group window.

Double-click the PC DOS Prompt icon to return temporarily to the PC DOS command prompt.

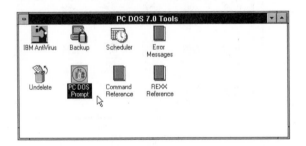

2. Double-click the PC DOS Prompt icon. You see the PC DOS command prompt displayed on-screen.

To return to Windows, follow these steps:

1. At the PC DOS command prompt, type **EXIT**.

2. Press **Enter**.

Note: *When Windows is running, do not type **WIN** to start it again.*

Chapter 5

Using File Manager

In Chapter 1, "Understanding System Basics," you learned how PC DOS uses files and directories to organize data on a disk. In Chapter 2, "Making PC DOS Work," you learned to use PC DOS commands to manage your files, directories, and disks.

Windows has a built-in program designed to help you visualize the organization of the information you have stored on disks. With Windows File Manager, you can view your disk organization on-screen and group your directories and files in an organization you can understand.

In this chapter, you learn to use File Manager to control your disks, files, and directories.

Opening the File Manager

The File Manager, like any other Windows application program, runs in its own window. You use the techniques covered in detail in Chapter 4, "Making Windows Work," to control the File Manager window.

To open the File Manager, follow these steps:

1. Double-click the Main group icon to open the window.

The File Manager
icon looks like a
two-drawer file
cabinet.

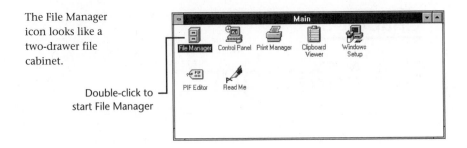

Double-click to
start File Manager

2. Double-click the File Manager icon. The File Manager opens.

Note: *To allow more space within the File Manager for viewing files,*
maximize the File Manager window.

The maximized
File Manager
window covers the
Program Manager
window on the
desktop.

Disk icons

Directory tree

Status line

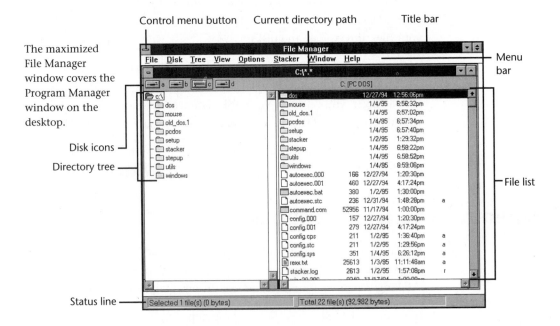

Control menu button   Current directory path   Title bar

Menu
bar

File list

At the top of the File Manager window, you see the title bar and the
menu bar. Below the menu bar, you see a window that displays icons
for the available drives, a directory list, and a file list. The name of the
current directory appears in the title bar of this window.

On the status line at the bottom of the File Manager window, you see the
number of bytes free, total bytes, and total number of files for the current
directory.

In the File Manager, directories are indicated by folder icons, and files are indicated by document icons. Program files are indicated by window icons.

The left side of the window shows the directory list and is called the Directory Tree area.

Selected directory

Folder icons

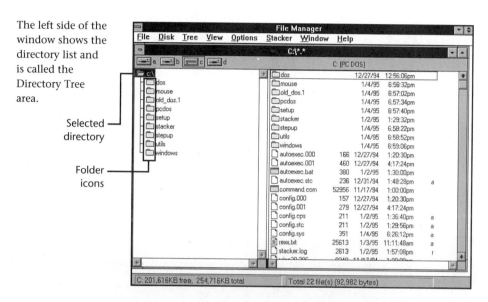

The right side of the window displays the subdirectories and files in the selected directory and is called the File List area.

Folder icons

Program icons

Document icons

Selected file

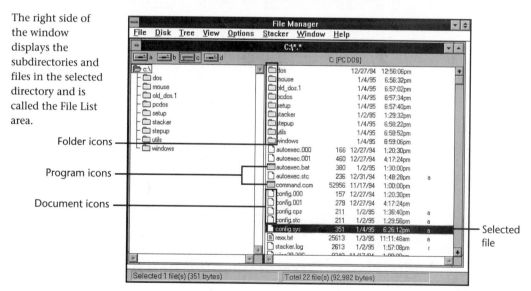

Note: *Your computer screen probably will look different from the screen used to illustrate this book because your hard disk will have different files and directories.*

Changing Drives

Active drive
The drive in which you currently are working.

In the File Manager, the Directory Tree area shows the directories stored on the *active drive*. If you want to work with directories and files stored on a different drive, you must change the active drive.

To make a different drive active, follow these steps:

1. Make sure that a diskette is in the drive you want to make active.

2. Click the diskette drive icon for the drive you want to make active. The Directory Tree and File List areas change to display the information on the diskette in the selected drive.

In this window, drive A is the active drive.

Drive icon ——

Current directory path ——

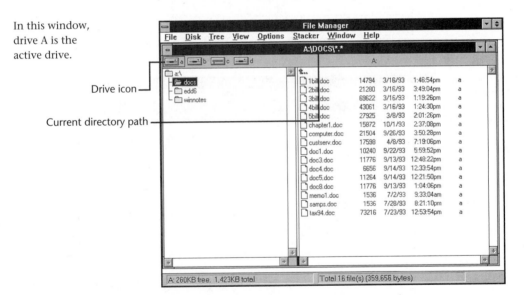

Opening Multiple Directory Windows

In the File Manager, you can open several directory windows at the same time. Each directory window can display different information. This capability is useful for seeing the contents of more than one directory or more than one disk.

To open an additional directory window, follow these steps:

1. Choose **W**indow from the menu bar to show the Window menu.

2. Choose **N**ew Window from the Window menu. A second window opens on top of the first window.

At first, the second window displays the same information as the first window. Later in this chapter, you learn how to change the information in the window.

New window

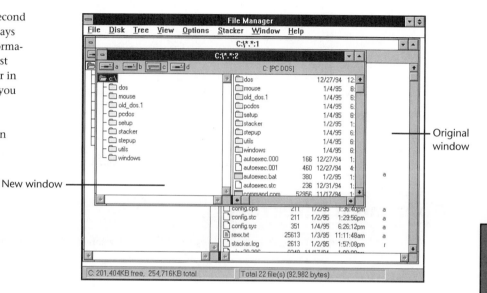

Original window

Note: *To quickly open an additional window, double-click the drive icon for the disk you want to be active in the new window.*

Arranging the Windows On-Screen

When you are working with more than one directory window open in the File Manager, you usually will want to be able to see the contents of all windows.

To arrange the windows on-screen so that you can see the contents of each, follow these steps:

1. Open the windows.

2. Choose **W**indow from the menu bar to show the Window menu.

3. Choose **T**ile from the Window menu.

You can tile the
windows on-screen
so that they do not
overlap.

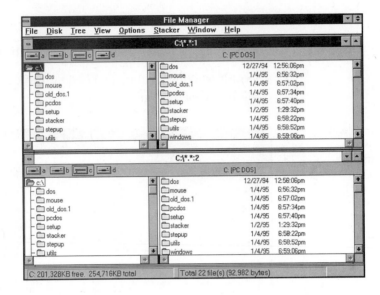

Opening a Directory

The File List area displays the files for the selected, or open, directory.

To open a directory, simply click the directory's folder icon in the directory tree. The folder icon opens, and the files contained in the directory are displayed in the File List area.

UTILS is the open
directory, and the
files and directo-
ries contained in
the UTILS
directory are
displayed.

Open folder icon

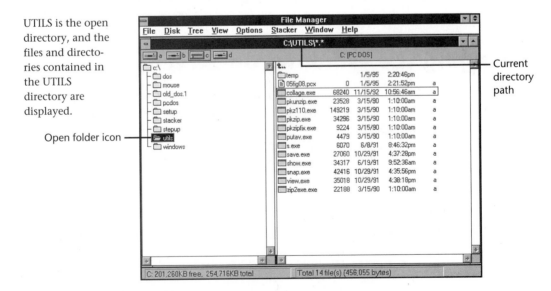

Current
directory
path

Expanding Directories

Expand

To display all the subdirectories for a selected directory or for the whole directory tree.

You can *expand* the directory tree to display subdirectories. You can expand only one directory, or you can expand all directories.

To expand a directory, double-click the directory's folder icon. The folder opens, and the subdirectories are displayed.

If you have problems...

If the folder opens but the subdirectories do not appear, you did not double-click fast enough. Try again.

The DOS directory has been expanded to display subdirectories.

PC DOS directory folder

Subdirectories

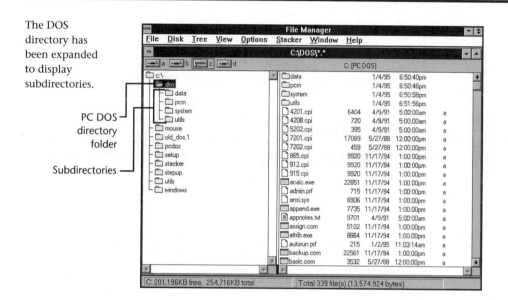

To expand all directories, follow these steps:

1. Choose **T**ree from the menu bar.

2. Choose Expand **A**ll from the Tree menu.

All directories and subdirectories on drive C are displayed in the Directory Tree area.

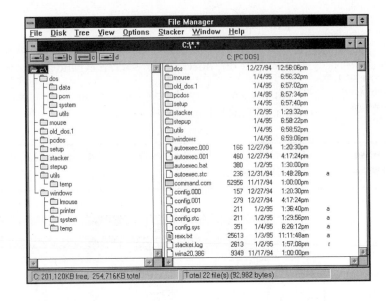

Collapsing Directories

Collapse

To hide subdirectories for a directory or directory tree.

You can *collapse* any expanded directory to hide the subdirectory folders.

To collapse a directory, double-click the directory's folder icon.

The root directory has been collapsed. All subdirectories of the root are hidden on the directory tree.

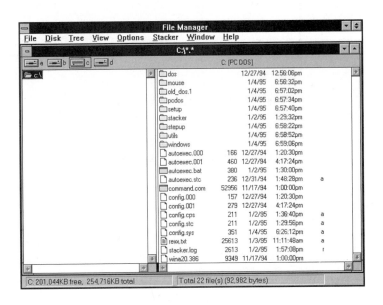

Changing the File Manager View

View
The way information in a utility or application program is displayed.

When you open the File Manager the first time, it appears in the default *view*. Both the directory tree and file list are displayed. You can change the way the File Manager displays information.

To change the File Manager view, follow these steps:

1. Choose **V**iew from the menu bar to show the View menu. The current view options are indicated on the View menu by check marks.

2. From the **V**iew menu, choose any of the following:

   ■ *Tree and Directory*. Displays both the directory tree and the file list. (This setting is the default.)

   ■ *Tree Only*. Displays only the Directory Tree area.

   ■ *Directory Only*. Displays only the File List area.

   ■ *Split*. Changes the location of the split between the File List area and the Directory Tree area. You can drag the split line to any location.

Note: *For more information on the other options on the View menu, see the next section, "Changing the File List."*

The view has been changed to display only the Directory Tree area.

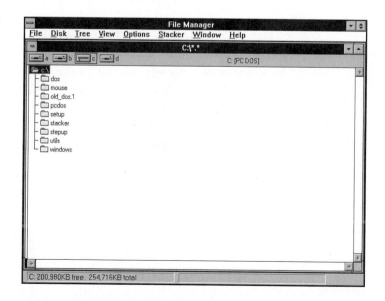

Changing the File List

You can change the file list in several ways: You can display only certain information about the files, you can sort the files in a different order, and you can display only certain files. The following sections explain how you can make these changes.

Displaying Specific Items of File Information

By default, the File Manager lists files alphabetically by name and displays all file information—including file name and extension, the time and date when the file was last modified, and the file size in bytes. You can choose what file information you want displayed.

To choose the file information you want displayed in the file list, follow these steps:

1. Choose **V**iew from the menu bar to show the View menu.

2. From the View menu, choose one of the following options:

   ■ *Name.* Displays only file names in the File List area.

   ■ *All File Details.* Displays all file information in the File List area.

   ■ *Partial Details.* Enables you to choose what file information you want to display.

File attribute

A term referring to four classifications of DOS files: hidden, read-only, archive, or system.

If you choose Partial Details, the Partial Details dialog box appears. In the Partial Details dialog box, you can choose to display file size; the last date the file was modified; the last time the file was modified; or the *file attributes*, including whether the file is a hidden file, a read-only file, an archived file, or a system file.

In the Partial Details dialog box, you can specify which file details you want to display.

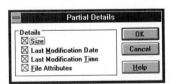

Sorting the File List

You can change the order of the file list. This feature is useful when you have many files and want certain files to appear near the top of the list.

To change the sort order of the files in the file list, follow these steps:

1. Choose **V**iew from the menu bar to show the View menu.

2. From the View menu, choose one of the following:

    ■ *Sort by Name.* Lists the files alphabetically by file name.

    ■ *Sort **b**y Type.* Lists files by type of file extension.

    ■ *Sort by Size.* Lists files according to size in bytes.

    ■ *Sort by **D**ate.* Lists files according to date stamp.

    ■ *By File **T**ype.* Displays only specified files. See the next section, "Displaying Specific Files," for more details.

In this window, the view has been changed to display only the File List area with the files sorted by size—from largest to smallest.

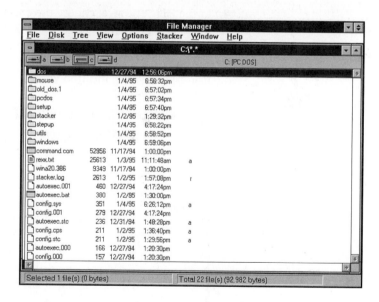

Displaying Specific Files

You can choose which files you want to include in the file list by using wild-card characters to specify a group of files.

To display only specified files, follow these steps:

1. Choose **V**iew from the menu bar to show the View menu.

2. Choose By File **T**ype from the View menu. The By File Type dialog box appears.

In the By File Type dialog box, you can specify the types of files you want to display.

Choose the file types ⎯

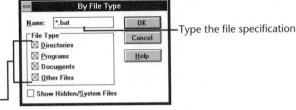

Type the file specification

3. In the **N**ame text box, type a file specification for the files you want to display. Use wild-card characters to specify a group of files. For example, type ***.TXT** to display all files with a TXT extension.

4. In the File Type area, choose the check boxes beside the types of files you want to display.

5. Click OK. The File List area changes to display only the files that match the file specification you entered.

In this window, only files matching the file specification *.bat are displayed.

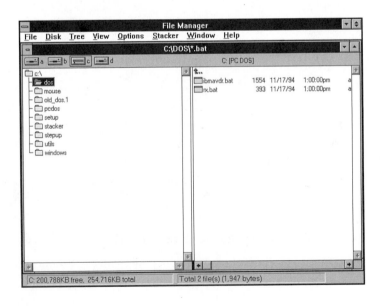

Searching for a File

If you forget where a file is located, you can use the File Manager to search for it. Even if you are not sure of the file name, you can use wildcard characters to find a group of files.

To search for a file, follow these steps:

1. Choose **F**ile, Searc**h**. The Search dialog box appears.

You can use the Search dialog box to search for a file anywhere on a disk.

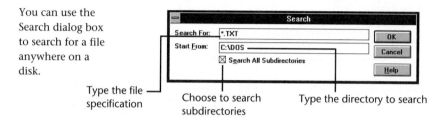

Type the file specification

Choose to search subdirectories

Type the directory to search

2. In the **S**earch For text box, type the name of the file you want to find, or use wild-card characters to specify a group of files.

3. In the Start **F**rom text box, type the name of the directory that you want to search. The box probably already shows the name of the current directory.

4. To search all subdirectories of the specified directory, make sure that the S**e**arch All Subdirectories check box has an x in it.

5. Choose OK. Windows looks for files that match the file specification.

When Windows completes the search, it displays the Search Results window. All the files that match the file specification are listed.

5

In the Search Results window, you see all the files that match the file specification you entered.

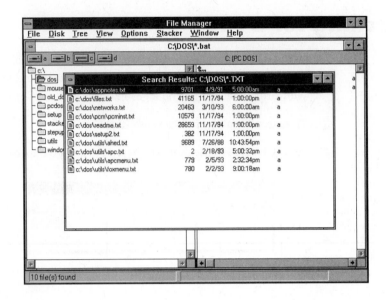

Note: *To close the Search Results window, double-click its Control menu button.*

Working with Files

You can use the File Manager to work with files in many ways. You must select a file before you can perform any action on it. After the file is selected, you can rename, move, copy, or delete it, as explained in the following sections.

Selecting Files

You can select one file or groups of files. Selected files are highlighted in the File List area.

To select a single file, click its icon in the File List area.

To select more than one file, follow these steps:

1. Click the icon of the first file you want to select.

2. Press and hold down **Ctrl**.

3. Click the icon of the next file you want to select.

4. Continue holding down **Ctrl** and clicking the icons to select the files.

5. When you have selected all the files you want, release the **Ctrl** key.

If you have problems...   If the first file you selected becomes unselected when you click another file, you are not holding down the Ctrl key. Try again.

Selected files are highlighted in the file list.

Selected files —

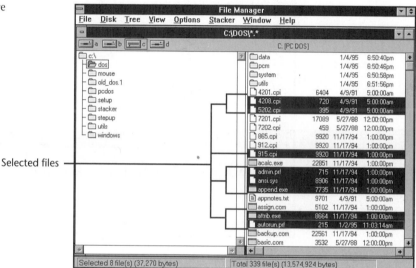

Copying Files

With two windows open on-screen, you easily can copy files from one location to another. You can copy files to another disk or to a different directory on the same disk.

To copy a file to another disk, follow these steps:

1. In one window, open the directory that contains the file you want to copy.

2. In another window, open the disk drive and the directory in which you want to place the copied file. Refer to the section "Opening Multiple Directory Windows," earlier in this chapter, for more information on displaying two directory windows.

3. Select the file you want to copy.

4. Drag the icon to the directory where you want to place the copied file. Notice that the file icon moves along with the mouse pointer. If you are copying more than one file, more than one file icon appears.

You can copy a file by dragging it from one directory window to another.

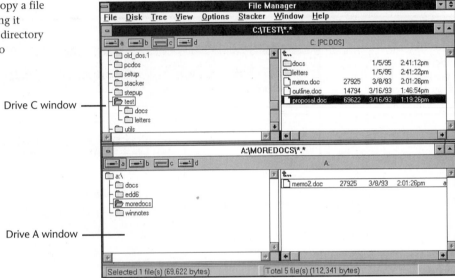

Drive C window —

Drive A window —

5. Release the mouse button. The File Manager displays the Confirm Mouse Operation dialog box.

6. Confirm that the file is being copied to the correct location, and then click Yes.

In the Confirm Mouse Operation dialog box, make sure that the file is being copied to the correct disk and directory.

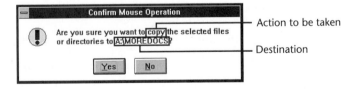

Action to be taken

Destination

To copy a file to a directory on the same disk, follow these steps:

1. In one window, open the directory that contains the file you want to copy.

2. In another window, make sure that the directory in which you want to place the copied file is displayed.

3. Select the file you want to copy.

4. Press and hold down **Ctrl**, and drag the icon to the directory where you want to place the copied file. Notice that the file icon moves with the mouse pointer. If you are copying more than one file, more than one file icon appears.

5. Release the mouse button. The File Manager displays the Confirm Mouse Operation dialog box.

6. Confirm that the file is being copied to the correct location, and then click **Yes**.

If you have problems...	If the Confirm Mouse Operation dialog box asks whether you want to move the file instead of copy it, you forgot to press and hold down Ctrl. To copy the file to a different directory on the same disk, you must press Ctrl before you drag the pointer.

5

Moving Files

You easily can move files from one location to another by dragging them from one directory window to another.

To move a file to a different disk, follow these steps:

1. In one window, open the directory that contains the file you want to move.

2. In another window, open the disk drive and the directory to which you want to move the file.

3. Select the file you want to move.

4. Press and hold down **Shift**, and drag the icon to the new location.

5. Release the mouse button. The Confirm Mouse Operation dialog box appears.

6. Confirm that the file is being moved to the correct location, and then click **Yes**.

If you have problems...   If the Confirm Mouse Operation dialog box asks whether you want to copy the file instead of move it, you forgot to press and hold down Shift. To move a file to a different disk, you must press and hold down Shift before you drag the file.

To move a file to a different directory on the same disk, follow these steps:

1. In one window, open the directory that contains the file you want to move.

2. In another window, make sure that the directory to which you want to move the file is displayed.

3. Select the file that you want to move.

4. Drag the icon to the new location.

5. Release the mouse button. The Confirm Mouse Operation dialog box appears.

6. Confirm that the file is being moved to the correct location, and then click **Yes**.

Deleting Files

With File Manager, you can delete a single file or a group of files. Because you see on-screen the files you are deleting, avoiding mistakes is easier than when deleting files from the PC DOS command prompt.

To delete a file, follow these steps:

1. Open the directory that contains the file you want to delete.

2. Select the file.

3. Choose **F**ile, **D**elete. The Delete dialog box appears.

Confirm the file name and the current directory name to make sure that you are deleting the correct file.

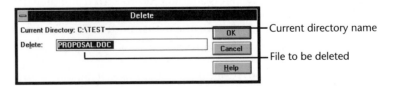

4. Click OK. The Confirm File Delete dialog box appears.

5. Confirm the file again, and then click **Yes**.

Note: *If you are deleting more than one file at a time and you are absolutely sure that all the files you have selected are correct, choose Yes to **A**ll in the Confirm File Delete dialog box. Then the File Manager will not prompt you to confirm each deletion.*

Renaming Files

To rename a file, follow these steps:

1. Open the directory that contains the file you want to rename.

2. Select the file you want to rename.

3. Choose **F**ile, Re**n**ame. The Rename dialog box appears, with the file name entered in the **F**rom text box.

Use the Rename
dialog box to
change the name
of a selected file.

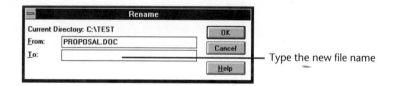

Type the new file name

4. In the **T**o text box, type the new file name.

5. Click OK.

Working with Directories

In File Manager, you easily can create, rename, move, or delete entire directories, as explained in the following sections.

Creating a Directory

To create a directory in File Manager, follow these steps:

1. Open the directory in which you want to create the new directory.

2. Choose **F**ile, **C**reate Directory. The Create Directory dialog box appears.

In the Create
Directory dialog
box, type a name
for the new
directory.

Type the new directory name

3. In the **N**ame text box, type a name for the new directory.

4. Click OK.

The new directory
appears in the
directory tree and
in the File List area
as a directory
within the current
directory.

New directory

**If you have
problems...**

If Windows displays a warning message telling you that the directory already
exists, you have tried to create a directory with the same name as an existing
directory. Click OK, and use a different directory name, or make the new
directory a subdirectory of a different directory.

Renaming a Directory

To rename a directory, follow these steps:

1. Select the directory you want to rename.

2. Choose **F**ile, Re**n**ame. The Rename dialog box appears, with the directory name already entered in the **F**rom text box.

You easily can rename an existing directory.

Type new directory name

Old directory name

3. In the **T**o text box, type the new directory name.

4. Click OK.

Moving a Directory

You can move a directory to a different disk, or you can make it a subdirectory of a different directory. When you move a directory, all the subdirectories and files it contains are moved with it.

To move a directory, follow these steps:

1. Select the directory you want to move.

2. Drag the directory to the new location. Notice that the folder icon moves with the mouse. The Confirm Mouse Operation dialog box appears.

3. Confirm that the directory is being moved to the correct location, and then click **Y**es.

Deleting Directories

When you delete a directory, all the subdirectories and files it contains are deleted as well.

To delete a directory, follow these steps:

1. Select the directory you want to delete.

2. Choose **F**ile, **D**elete. The Delete dialog box appears.

In the Delete dialog box, confirm that the directory specified in the Delete text box is the one you want to delete.

3. Click OK. The Confirm Directory Delete dialog box appears.

4. Confirm that the specified directory is the one you want to delete, and then choose **Yes**.

Note: *If the directory you are deleting contains files or subdirectories, Windows asks you to confirm each deletion. To delete all the files and subdirectories without confirmation, choose Yes to All in the Confirm Delete dialog box.*

Formatting Diskettes

You can use the File Manager to format diskettes in drive A or drive B.

To format diskettes, follow these steps:

1. Insert the diskette you want to format into the diskette drive.

2. Choose **Disk**, **Format Disk**. The Format Disk dialog box appears.

In the Format Disk dialog box, specify the capacity and location of the diskette you want to format.

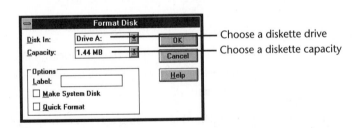

Choose a diskette drive
Choose a diskette capacity

Caution

Formatting wipes out all existing data. Use a blank diskette, or be sure you do not need the existing files on the diskette.

3. If necessary, click the drop-down arrow next to the **Disk** In text box to choose the diskette drive where the diskette is located.

4. If necessary, click the drop-down arrow next to the **Capacity** text box to choose the capacity of the diskette to be formatted.

5. Click OK. The Confirm Format Disk dialog box appears, reminding you that all existing data on the disk will be erased.

6. Click **Y**es to begin formatting the disk.

When the format is complete, you see a message asking whether you want to format another diskette. Click **Y**es to format another. Click **N**o to return to the File Manager window.

Copying a Diskette

You can use the File Manager to copy a diskette's contents to another diskette that is the same size and capacity. If you have two diskette drives of the same size, you can put the source diskette in one drive and the destination diskette in the other drive. If you have only one diskette drive or if you have two diskette drives of different sizes, you can use one diskette drive.

Note: *You can, of course, copy files and directories from one disk or diskette to another that is not the same size and capacity. However, to copy the entire diskette, both the source and the destination diskettes must be the same size and capacity.*

To copy a diskette, follow these steps:

1. Choose **D**isk, **C**opy Disk. The Copy Disk dialog box appears.

You can copy the information on a diskette to a diskette of the same size and capacity.

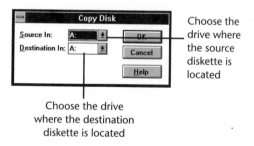

Choose the drive where the source diskette is located

Choose the drive where the destination diskette is located

2. If necessary, click the drop-down arrow next to the **S**ource In text box, and choose the drive into which you will insert the diskette you want to copy.

3. If necessary, click the drop-down arrow next to the **D**estination In text box, and choose the drive into which you will insert the blank diskette.

4. Click OK. The Confirm Copy Disk dialog box appears, reminding you that all the existing data on the destination disk will be erased by the copy procedure.

5. Click **Y**es. The Copy Disk dialog box appears, prompting you to insert the source diskette.

6. Insert the diskette you want to copy into the correct drive.

7. Click OK. The copy process begins.

   At the appropriate time, the File Manager prompts you to insert the destination diskette into the correct drive and to click OK to continue. You may need to change diskettes more than once.

8. When the diskette is copied, the File Manager asks whether you want to copy another. Choose **Y**es to copy another diskette. Choose **N**o to return to the File Manager window.

Starting an Application Program from the File Manager

In Chapter 4, "Making Windows Work," you learned several ways to start application programs from the Program Manager. You also can start application programs directly from the File Manager.

Note: *Application programs are started using executable files. Executable files usually are identified by one of three file extensions: EXE, COM, or BAT. To determine the name of the executable file used to start a particular application program, consult the application program's documentation.*

To start an application program from the File Manager, follow these steps:

1. Open the directory that contains the program files for the application program you want to start.

2. Double-click the file that starts the application program. The program starts.

You can start
an application
program from the
File Manager by
double-clicking
the file that runs
the application
program. Here,
IBMAVD.EXE is
the executable file
used to start IBM
AntiVirus for DOS.

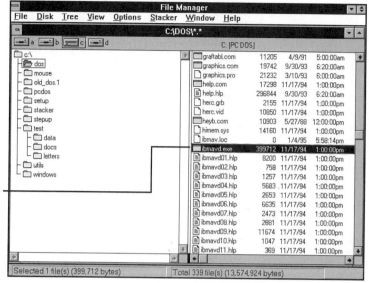

Double-click the
EXE file to start
the application
program

If you do not know which file runs the application program, consult your
application program documentation. Usually, application program files have
EXE extensions. The file PBRUSH.EXE, for example, starts and runs the Paintbrush program.

**If you have
problems...**

Changing the File Manager Font

Font

A specific size and
style of character
that can be printed
or displayed on a
computer.

If you want to change the appearance of the File Manager on-screen, you
can change the *font* used to display characters.

To change the File Manager font, follow these steps:

1. Choose **O**ptions on the menu bar to show the Options menu.

2. Choose **F**ont from the Options menu. The Font dialog box appears.

In the Font dialog box, you can choose the font, font style, and font size you want displayed in the File Manager.

Choose a font ⎯

Choose a font style ⎯

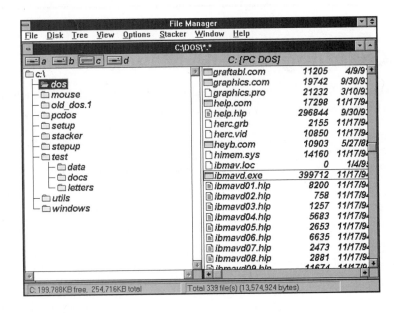

Choose a font size

Preview the font

3. In the **F**ont list, select the font you want to use. You can preview a sample of the font in the Sample area.

4. In the Font St**y**le list, select the font style you want to use.

5. In the **S**ize list, select the font size you want to use.

   Note: *Fonts are measured in points; 72 points equal one inch. The larger the point size, the larger the font characters.*

6. To display both uppercase and lowercase characters, choose the **L**owercase check box so that it shows an x.

7. Choose OK. The File Manager display changes.

The File Manager font here is 12-point boldface italic Arial.

Closing the File Manager

You use the same methods to close the File Manager that you use to close any Windows application program.

To close the File Manager, double-click the Control menu button at the left end of the File Manager title bar.

If you have problems...	If you double-click the Control menu button but nothing happens, you probably are double-clicking the directory window Control menu button, not the File Manager Control menu button. Be sure to click the Control menu button at the left end of the File Manager title bar.

5

Part II
Beyond the Basics

Chapter 6

Customizing Your Desktop

In Windows, the Control Panel enables you to customize the way your mouse, keyboard, screen, and desktop work. When you change an option in the Control Panel, the change remains in effect until you change the setting again—even after you leave Windows.

In this chapter, you learn how to use the Control Panel to set the system date and time, customize the mouse, customize the keyboard, customize the desktop, and customize the screen.

Starting the Control Panel

The Control Panel is in the Program Manager's Main group. To start the Control Panel, double-click the Control Panel program icon.

The icons in the Control Panel window represent settings you can customize in Windows.

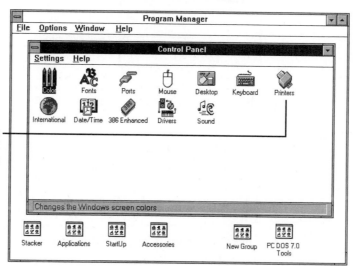

Double-click an icon to change a Control Panel setting

If you have problems...	Your Control Panel may not have exactly the same icons as the ones shown in the illustrations for this chapter. You probably have additional icons if you have installed other devices, such as an extra pointing device, or if you are on a network.

Changing the System Date and Time

When you use your computer to create a file or to save a document, PC DOS marks the file with the date and time you saved it or updated it. This information, displayed when you view a directory listing in the File Manager or from the PC DOS command prompt, is helpful when you want to find the most recent version of a file or you want to check when you typed a report.

You can change the date and time whenever you need to, such as if you change to daylight savings time or if you move to a new time zone.

To change your computer's system date and time, follow these steps:

1. Open the Control Panel window.

2. Double-click the Date/Time icon. The Date & Time dialog box appears.

In the Date & Time dialog box, you can change the system date and time.

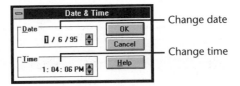

3. Click the part of the date or time that is incorrect. The insertion point moves to that spot.

4. Click the up- or down-arrow button to the right of the date or time until the setting is correct, or use the keyboard to type the correct number.

5. Repeat steps 3 and 4 to change other parts of the time and date.

6. Click OK when the date and time are correct.

Customizing the Mouse

You can control how fast the mouse pointer moves across the screen, how fast you need to double-click, and even which mouse button functions as the left button. You also can turn on the Mouse Trails feature, which traces the movements of the mouse pointer on-screen.

To customize the mouse settings, follow these steps:

1. Open the Control Panel window.

2. Double-click the Mouse icon. The Mouse dialog box appears.

Click for faster tracking speed

You can customize the mouse settings to control the way the mouse responds.

Click to slow double-click speed

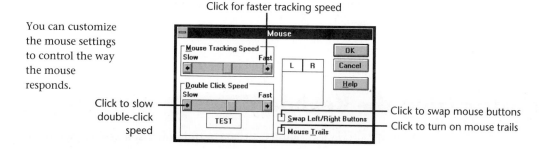

Click to swap mouse buttons
Click to turn on mouse trails

3. In the **M**ouse Tracking Speed area, take one of the following steps:

■ Click the arrow under the word `Fast` to increase the speed with which the mouse pointer responds to mouse movements.

■ Click the arrow under the word `Slow` to decrease the speed with which the mouse pointer responds to mouse movements.

4. In the **D**ouble Click Speed area, take one of the following actions:

■ Click the arrow under the word `Fast` to increase the speed with which the mouse responds to a double-click. (This setting means that you must double-click faster in order for the mouse to respond.)

■ Click the arrow under the word `Slow` to decrease the speed with which the mouse responds to a double-click. (This setting means that you can double-click more slowly and still get a response.)

6

Note: *You can test the double-click speed to see whether it is comfortable for you to use. Double-click the TEST box. If it turns darker, the mouse registered the double-click. If the TEST box does not turn darker, you are clicking too fast or too slow. Adjust the speed and try again.*

5. Click the check box next to **S**wap Left/Right Buttons if you want to use the right mouse button to register left mouse button clicks, and the left mouse button to register right mouse button clicks. This option is useful particularly if you are left-handed and want to do most of your clicking with the index finger on your left hand.

6. Click the check box next to Mouse **T**rails if you want the mouse to leave a trail across the screen as it moves.

7. Choose OK to accept the settings and return to the Control Panel window.

Customizing the Keyboard

The Keyboard option enables you to control how fast a key repeats when you press and hold it down. In addition, you can specify how long your computer waits while you hold down a key before that key repeats.

To customize your keyboard, follow these steps:

1. Open the Control Panel window.

2. Double-click the Keyboard icon. The Keyboard dialog box appears.

You can set and test your keyboard response time in the Keyboard dialog box.

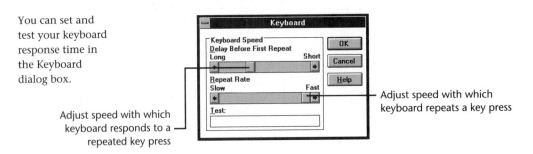

Adjust speed with which keyboard responds to a repeated key press

Adjust speed with which keyboard repeats a key press

3. In the **D**elay Before First Repeat area, take one of the following actions:

   ■ Click the arrow under the word Short to decrease the amount of time between the first response to a key press and a repeat of the action if you do not release the key.

   ■ Click the arrow under the word Long to increase the amount of time between the first response to a key press and a repeat of the action if you do not release the key. This option gives you more time to release the key before the keyboard repeats the action.

4. In the **R**epeat Rate area, take one of the following actions:

   ■ Click the arrow under the word Fast to increase the speed with which the keyboard repeats an action if you hold down the key.

   ■ Click the arrow under the word Slow to decrease the speed with which the keyboard repeats an action if you hold down the key. This option gives you more time to release the key without repeating the action.

5. Click OK to accept the settings and return to the Control Panel window.

Note: *You can test the keyboard response rates by using the **T**est area in the Keyboard dialog box. Click within the **T**est box; then press and hold down any key. You can see how long it takes for the keyboard to register the key press and then how quickly (or slowly) the keyboard repeats the key press.*

Choosing a Color Scheme

By now, you probably have noticed that different elements in Windows appear in different colors. The title bar is one color, the menu bar another, selected text another, menu text still another, and so on. Windows gives you a wide variety of different color schemes from which you can choose to give your Windows programs the look you want.

6

To choose a preset color scheme, follow these steps:

1. Open the Control Panel window.

2. Double-click the Color icon. The Color dialog box appears.

You can select a preset color scheme, or you can create your own using the Color palette.

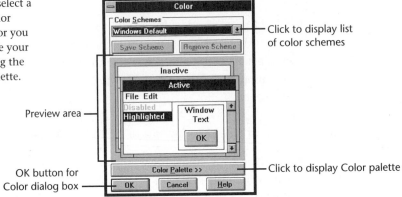

Preview area

OK button for Color dialog box

Click to display list of color schemes

Click to display Color palette

3. Click the arrow in the Color **S**chemes text box to drop down a list of color schemes.

4. Click a color scheme from the list. The selected colors appear in the preview area.

5. Choose OK to accept the selected color scheme.

If you have problems...

If you click OK and nothing happens, you may be clicking the OK button in the preview area. That button shows you only the color that buttons will have. The actual OK button for the Color dialog box is on the bottom line of the box.

Creating a Custom Color Scheme

You can pick and choose a certain color for each element of Windows, giving your Windows programs a unique appearance. You can change an existing color scheme or create a new color scheme by assigning new colors to many parts of the Windows screen.

To create your own color scheme, follow these steps:

1. Open the Control Panel window.

2. Double-click the Color icon to display the Color dialog box.

3. Choose Color **P**alette from the Color dialog box.

You can customize
the Windows
colors by choosing
colors from the
Color palette.

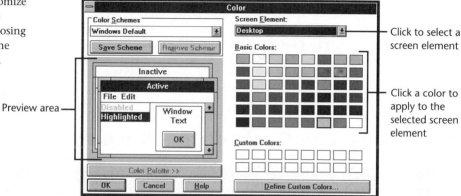

Click to select a
screen element

Click a color to
apply to the
selected screen
element

Preview area

4. From the Color **S**chemes drop-down list, choose a color scheme to use as a basis for the new color scheme.

If you have problems...   Don't worry about altering an existing color scheme. You can save your changes as a new scheme with a different name and avoid affecting the existing color scheme.

6

5. Click the arrow next to the Screen **E**lement text box to drop down a list of screen elements.

6. Select the part of the screen you want to change.

7. In the **B**asic Colors palette, click the color you want the screen element to be. The preview area reflects your change.

8. Repeat steps 5 through 7 to change the colors of other screen elements until you like the overall appearance of the screen in the preview area.

9. Choose S**a**ve Scheme to save the new color scheme. The Save Scheme dialog box appears.

In the Save
Scheme dialog
box, you can type
a name for your
color scheme.

Caution

If you do not type a
new name, the
changes are made
to the current color
scheme.

10. In the text box of the Save Scheme dialog box, type a new name for the color scheme.

11. Choose OK in the Save Scheme dialog box.

12. Choose OK in the Color dialog box to return to the Control Panel window.

Changing the Desktop Background

Wallpaper

A drawing or
scanned picture
used for the desk-
top background.

One way to modify the appearance of Windows is to change the desktop background. You can add patterns and *wallpaper*, and you can turn on a screen saver to prolong the life of your display. To change the appearance of the desktop, use the Desktop dialog box.

To open the Desktop dialog box, follow these steps:

1. Open the Control Panel window.

2. Double-click the Desktop icon. The Desktop dialog box appears.

You can change
many aspects of
the Windows
desktop by
changing the
settings in the
Desktop dialog
box.

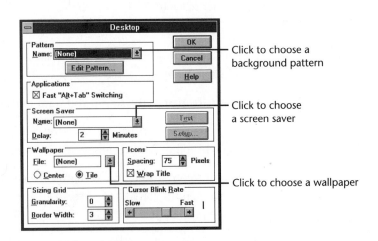

Click to choose a
background pattern

Click to choose
a screen saver

Click to choose a wallpaper

Customizing the Desktop Pattern

To change the desktop pattern, follow these steps:

1. Double-click the Desktop icon in the Control Panel window to open the Desktop dialog box.

2. In the Pattern area, click the arrow next to the **N**ame text box to drop down a list of pattern names.

3. Select a pattern from the list.

4. Choose Edit **P**attern to view the pattern.

5. Choose OK to return to the Desktop dialog box.

6. Choose OK to return to the Control Panel.

Note: *To get a clear view of the new pattern, minimize the Program Manager so that the desktop appears without any windows open.*

The Desktop pattern has been changed to Quilt.

If you have problems...   Using a pattern requires a great deal of system memory. If you add a pattern and your system runs very slowly, change the Desktop pattern back to None.

Customizing the Wallpaper

Instead of using a pattern for the desktop, you can use a drawing or scanned picture—wallpaper—for your background. Windows includes several wallpapers you can use, or you can create your own.

If you have problems...

Using wallpaper requires a great deal of system memory. If you add wallpaper and your system runs very slowly, change the Wallpaper option back to None.

To customize the Desktop wallpaper, follow these steps:

1. Double-click the Desktop icon in the Control Panel window to open the Desktop dialog box.

2. In the Wallpaper area, click the arrow next to the **F**ile text box to drop down a list of available wallpapers.

If you have problems...

If no files appear in the Wallpaper list, you have no files with BMP extensions in the Windows directory. You can reinstall Windows to replace the BMP files.

---

3. Select a file from the list.

4. Select the **T**ile option to apply the wallpaper evenly across the desktop. Choose the **C**enter option to display one graphic image in the center of your screen.

5. Choose OK to close the Desktop dialog box. The wallpaper appears on the desktop.

The ARCADE.BMP file is used to wallpaper the desktop.

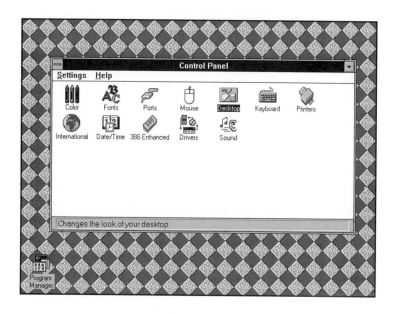

Using a Screen Saver

Screen saver
A program that displays a changing image on your display to reduce the possibility of image burn-in.

If you leave Windows on for a very long time, sooner or later it may burn a faint image on your display screen. You will see the image even when the display is turned off or when you are working from the PC DOS command prompt. To avoid this problem, you can turn off Windows when you are not using it, or you can use a *screen saver*.

To turn on a Windows screen saver, follow these steps:

1. Double-click the Desktop icon from the Control Panel to open the Desktop dialog box.

2. In the Screen Saver area, click the arrow next to the Name box to drop down the list of available screen savers.

3. Choose a screen saver from the list.

4. In the Delay text box, enter the length of time you want the computer to remain idle before Windows starts the screen saver.

5. Choose Test to view the screen saver. To end the test, move the mouse.

6. Choose OK.

6

Chapter 7

Working with the Text Editor

ASCII file
A file that contains alphanumeric and control characters, such as text. AUTOEXEC.BAT is an example of an ASCII file.

PC DOS comes with the E Editor, a full-screen text editor that enables you to create, edit, and print memos, letters, and *ASCII files* quickly and easily.

The version of the E Editor that comes with PC DOS 7.0 has been enhanced significantly. Most notably, it has menu commands for most command functions, and you can use a mouse to make selections and mark text.

This chapter introduces you to the E Editor. You learn the basics of starting the E Editor and of using it to create, modify, and print a text file.

Starting the E Editor

You can start the E Editor from the PC DOS command prompt, from a Shell program such as the PC DOS Shell, or from Windows. The file used to start the E Editor is E.EXE.

To start the E Editor from the PC DOS command prompt, type **E** and press **Enter**. If you want to open a particular file, type **E**, press the **spacebar** once, type the file name, and press **Enter**.

To start the E Editor from Windows, follow these steps:

1. Choose **F**ile, **R**un in the Program Manager window. The Run dialog box appears.

One way to start the E Editor is from the Windows Program Manager.

Type the command line

Click OK to start the E Editor

2. In the **C**ommand Line text box, type the file specification for the E.EXE file. For example, type **C:\DOS\E.EXE**.

3. Click OK. The E Editor starts, and a full-screen window opens.

To start the E Editor from the File Manager, open the DOS directory folder and double-click the E.EXE file in the File List area. Or, you can add a program item for the E Editor to the PC DOS 7.0 Tools program group and then start the E Editor from that group. For information on starting programs and adding items to a program group, see Chapter 4, "Making Windows Work."

Understanding the E Editor

The E Editor creates and saves unformatted, or ASCII, text files. ASCII files contain only text characters and a few control characters you can enter on your keyboard, such as tabs and returns.

Cursor
A marker indicating where text will appear when you type.

The E Editor provides a full-screen window for entering text. Characters that you type on your keyboard appear at the *cursor* location, between the top-of-file and bottom-of-file markers.

Top-of-file marker   Text entry area   Menu line

If you do not open
an existing file, the
E Editor starts with
a blank, unnamed
file open in a full-
screen window.

Bottom-of-
file marker

```
File  Edit  Macro  Search  View  Options  Help
===== Top of file =====
===== Bottom of file =====
```

File name
Status line
Reminder line

```
.Unnamed file                          Line      1 Col      1  Insert    E 3.13U
F1=Help  2=Save   3=Close  4=File  5=Print        7=Rename  8=Open  9=Undo  10=Menu
```

Command
line

The E Editor status line near the bottom of the screen indicates the file name as well as the text line number, the column number, and whether Insert mode is turned on.

**E Editor
command line**
An area in the E
Editor window
where you can
enter text-editing
commands.

Function keys
Special command
keys on your key-
board that are
labeled with the
letter *F* and a
number.

The line above the status line is the *E Editor command line.* You can use the command line to perform E Editor commands such as naming a file.

The line at the very top of the screen is the E Editor menu line. You can choose commands from menus with a mouse.

At the bottom of the screen is the Reminder line, also called the function key text area. The actions associated with the *function keys* are displayed on the Reminder line.

The function keys enable you to perform most E Editor tasks with only one keystroke. You can press the Alt, Shift, or Scroll key to display additional function keys. Table 7.1 lists the basic E Editor function keys and their associated actions.

7

Table 7.1 E Editor Function Keys	
Key	**Action**
F1	Displays on-line Help.
F2	Saves the text file you are editing without closing the file.
F3	Exits the E Editor and returns to the PC DOS Shell without saving the file. If changes have been made since the last save, the E Editor asks whether you want to exit without saving. From the on-line Help, F3 returns to the E Editor.
F4	Saves the current file and exits the E Editor.
F6	Shows the options for drawing text graphics.
F7	Changes the current file name.
F8	Opens the specified file for editing without closing the current file.
F9	Cancels editing changes made to the current line.
F10	Displays the next open file for editing without closing the current file.

Creating a Text File

Word wrap
The way text automatically moves down to the beginning of the next line when the current line is filled.

To create a text file, just type your text in the E Editor window. E Editor does not have *word wrap*, so you must press **Enter** to move the cursor to the next line. You can type up to 254 characters plus a carriage return on each line in the E Editor.

Note: *You can set margins in the E Editor to simulate word wrap.*

If you have problems...

If you do not press **Enter** when your text reaches the edge of the screen, the line continues to scroll to the right, and the characters at the beginning of the line disappear off the left side of the screen. Press the **left-arrow** key to scroll back to the beginning of the line, or press **Home**.

You can use the cursor-control keys to move within the file as you type or to view parts of the file that already have been entered. If you have a mouse, you can click the mouse to move the cursor, also. Table 7.2 lists the cursor-control keys and their functions.

Table 7.2 E Editor Cursor-Control Keys	
Key	**Action**
Up arrow	Moves up one line.
Down arrow	Moves down one line.
Left arrow	Moves left one character.
Right arrow	Moves right one character.
Home	Moves to column 1 of the current line.
End	Moves to the last character of the current line.
PgUp	Moves up one page of text.
PgDn	Moves down one page of text.
Ctrl+Home	Moves to the first line in the file.
Ctrl+End	Moves to the last line in the file.
Ctrl+PgUp	Moves to the first line of the current screen.
Ctrl+PgDn	Moves to the last line of the current screen.
Ctrl+left arrow	Moves to the first character of the word on which the cursor currently is positioned.
Ctrl+right arrow	Moves to the last character of the word on which the cursor currently is positioned.
Ctrl+Enter	Moves to column 1 of the next line.
Tab	Moves to the next tab stop.
Shift+Tab	Moves to the preceding tab stop.
Esc	Toggles to and from the E Editor command line.

Editing with the E Editor

7

The PC DOS E Editor is a powerful line editor that contains many of the same features found in high-end word processors. With just one or two keystrokes, you can perform most editing tasks, including inserting, deleting, moving, and copying blocks of text.

Entering Text in a File

When you open a new file in the E Editor, you can begin typing your new document. If you open an existing file, you can immediately make changes.

The E Editor is a line editor, which means that you must manually insert line breaks, or line feeds, as you type.

To insert a line break, simply press **Enter** at the point where you want to end the current line and start a new line. The cursor moves to the beginning of the next line.

In the E Editor, you must manually insert line breaks by pressing Enter.

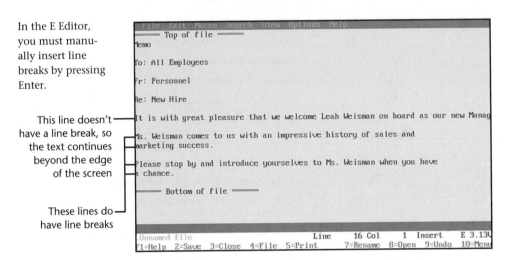

This line doesn't have a line break, so the text continues beyond the edge of the screen

These lines do have line breaks

If you try later to insert a line break in an existing line of text by pressing Enter, you will see that a new line is inserted between the current line of text and the next line; the original line of text remains intact. Furthermore, you cannot remove a line feed by pressing Backspace or Delete.

If you did not insert a line break when you first typed a line of text, you can go back and split the line.

To split an existing line of text into two separate lines, follow these steps:

1. Position the cursor on the character you want as the first character of the new line.

2. Choose **E**dit, **S**plit Line or press **Alt+S**. A new line is inserted in the file, and the text from the cursor location to the end of the line is moved to the beginning of the new line. The cursor remains in its previous position, which is now the end of the original line.

If you have problems...

If the new line begins with a space, you had the cursor positioned on a space between two words. Be sure to position the cursor on the character with which you want to begin the new line before you press **Alt+S**.

To remove a line break and join two consecutive lines into one line, follow these steps:

1. Position the cursor anywhere on the first line.

2. Choose **E**dit, **J**oin Lines or press **Alt+J**. The line break at the end of the line on which the cursor is located is removed, automatically joining the two lines into one. Now the line probably extends past the edge of the viewing area.

Adding Text to a File

Insert mode

A setting that tells the E Editor to insert new text at the cursor location, pushing existing text to the right.

Replace mode

A setting that tells the E Editor to replace, or over-write, existing text.

To add text to a file, simply position the cursor where you want the text to appear and begin typing. By default, the E Editor opens in *Insert mode*. As you type, text is inserted into the file at the cursor location.

If you want to overwrite existing text, change to *Replace mode* by pressing the Insert key on your keyboard. Text that you type replaces existing text at the cursor location.

E Editor has two ways of indicating the mode in which it currently is working:

■ *The status line.* The word `Insert` indicates Insert mode. The word `Replace` indicates Replace mode.

■ *The cursor.* A rectangular cursor indicates Insert mode. An underline indicates Replace mode.

7

If the word `Insert` appears on the status line and the cursor is a rectangular shape, the E Editor is in Insert mode.

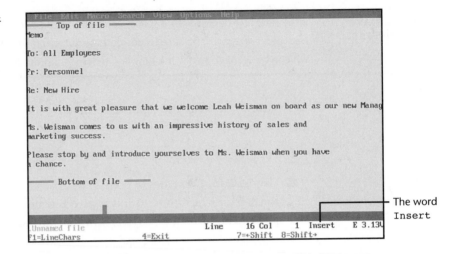

The word `Insert`

If the word `Replace` appears on the status line and the cursor is an underline, the E Editor is in Replace mode.

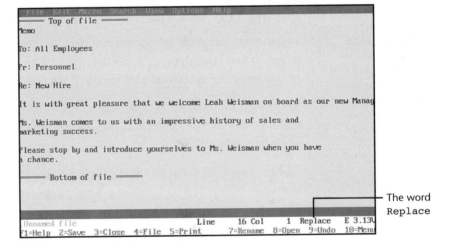

The word `Replace`

Deleting Text from a File

With the E Editor, you can remove text one character at a time, one word at a time, or one line at a time.

To remove text one character at a time, take one of the following actions:

- Press **Delete** to remove the character on which the cursor currently is located.

- Press **Backspace** to remove the character to the left of the cursor.

To remove text one word at a time, follow these steps:

1. Position the cursor at the beginning of the word you want to delete.

2. Press **Ctrl+D**. The characters from the cursor to the end of the word are deleted.

To remove an entire line of text, follow these steps:

1. Position the cursor anywhere on the line you want to delete.

2. Choose **E**dit, **D**elete Line or press **Ctrl+Backspace**. The entire line is deleted, and the text below the deleted line moves up one line.

If you have problems...	If you realize that you have made a mistake, you can undo the change immediately by pressing **F9**, or by choosing **E**dit, **U**ndo. To undelete a line immediately after deleting it, choose **E**dit, **U**ndelete Line or press **Ctrl+U**.

Marking Text

Mark
To select text
in a file.

With the E Editor, you can manipulate the contents of a file by *marking* the text. You can mark text by using the keyboard or a mouse, or by choosing menu commands. After you mark the text, you can perform such functions as copying, moving, or deleting.

In a single line, you can mark any amount of text from a single character to the entire line. You also can mark several lines, a rectangular block, or the entire file. No matter how much text is marked, the marked area appears highlighted on-screen.

To mark a single character, or a series of characters not in a block or a line, follow these steps:

1. Position the cursor on the character you want to mark.

2. Press **Alt+Z** or choose **E**dit, **M**ark Text.

To mark a word, follow these steps:

1. Position the cursor anywhere within the word you want to mark.

2. Press **Alt+W** or click the right mouse button.

7

Note: *If the cursor is positioned on a space when you press **Alt+W**, the E Editor marks the next word to the right of the cursor. If there is no word to the right, it marks the next word to the left of the cursor. If there are no words at all on the current line, the E Editor marks the current space character.*

To mark an entire line, follow these steps:

1. Position the cursor anywhere within the line you want to mark.

2. Press **Alt+L** or choose **E**dit, Mark **L**ine.

You can use the mouse to quickly mark lines of text. Just press and hold the right mouse button, and drag the mouse pointer across the lines you want to mark.

To mark a block of text, follow these steps:

1. Position the cursor anywhere within the first line you want to mark.

2. Choose **E**dit, Mark B**l**ock or press **Alt+L**.

3. Move the cursor to the last line of text that you want to mark.

4. Choose **E**dit, Mark B**l**ock or press **Alt+L**.

The E Editor marks the first and last lines and all the lines between them.

To mark a rectangular block of text, follow these steps:

1. Position the cursor on the character that will be in the upper left corner of the rectangular block.

2. Press **Alt+B**.

3. Position the cursor on the character that will be in the lower right corner of the rectangular block.

4. Press **Alt+B** again.

Note: *Marking rectangular blocks of text is useful particularly when you are working with columns of data. It is important to note, however, that when you copy or move a rectangular block of data, you must place the block into blank space, or it will overwrite any existing data.*

A rectangular block of text has been marked and is highlighted on-screen.

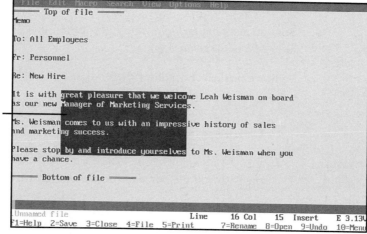

Marked block of text

To unmark any text, press **Alt+U** or double-click on the marked area. To delete marked text, press **Alt+D**.

Copying Text

Copy

To place an exact copy of marked text at a different location.

You can *copy* marked text to a new location in the same file or in another file without affecting the original text.

To copy text, follow these steps:

1. Open the file that contains the text you want to copy.

2. Mark the text you want to copy.

3. If you want to copy the text to another file, press **F8** and type the path and file name of the other file without closing the original file.

4. Position the cursor at the location where you want to insert the copied text. If you need to switch from one open file to the other, press **F10** to switch.

5. Choose **E**dit, **C**opy Marked Area or press **Alt+C** to copy the text.

Note: *The E Editor stores marked text in a temporary storage area. Until you mark different text, you can press **Alt+C** as many times as you want to insert the text into several locations.*

7

Moving Text

Move

To move the marked text from one location to another location.

You can *move* marked text from one location in a file to another location or from one file to another.

To move marked text, follow these steps:

1. Open the file that contains the text you want to move.

2. Mark the text you want to move.

3. If you want to move the text to a different file, press **F8** and type the path and file name of the file without closing the original file.

4. Position the cursor at the location where you want to insert the text. If you want to switch from one open file to another, press **F10**.

5. Choose **E**dit, **M**ove Marked Area or press **Alt+M**. The E Editor moves the text from its original location to the current cursor location. The existing text moves to allow for the insertion.

Naming and Saving a File with the E Editor

Before you can save a file with the E Editor, the file must have a name.

Note: *You can name a file at any time.*

To name and save a file, follow these steps:

1. Choose **F**ile, **R**ename or press **F7**, the Name function key. The cursor moves down to the E Editor command line. You enter the Name command there.

2. Type the file name. Remember to include the complete path. If you do not include the complete path, the file will be saved in the current directory.

3. Press **Enter**. The name appears below the command line.

4. Press **F4** to save the file and exit the E Editor.

Press F7 and enter
the complete path
and file name on
the E Editor
command line. In
this example, the
file MEMO.TXT is
stored in the
\DATA
subdirectory.

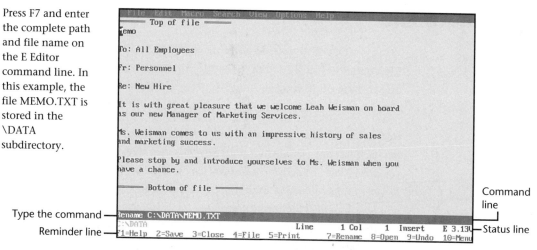

Type the command ⎯
Reminder line ⎯

Command
line

Status line

After you press
Enter, the path
and file name
appear on the
status line. Press
Esc to move the
cursor back to the
text area if you
want to continue
working with the
file.

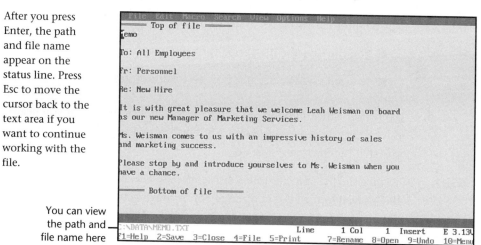

You can view
the path and ⎯
file name here

7

You also can use the Rename command to save a new version of the
current file with a new name. Renaming the current file doesn't change
the name of the previous version of the file already stored on your disk.
To rename an existing file, follow the same procedure used for naming a
new file. Press **Esc** to return to the text area, and continue editing the file
with its new name.

Saving a File

When you have completed entering or editing text, you must save the file. Actually, you should save the file periodically, even while you still are working on it. If something happens to disrupt your computer session, you will still have a fairly recent version of the file saved.

Note: *The E Editor has an Autosave feature that automatically saves the file in which you are working at regular intervals, based on the number of times you press Enter. To activate Autosave, choose* **O***ptions,* **A***utosave (or, press* **Esc** *to move to the command line and type* **AUTOSAVE***), press the* **spacebar***, and type a number indicating how many times you want to press Enter before the file is saved. If you type* **AUTOSAVE 10***, for example, the E Editor saves your file after you press* **Enter** *10 times.*

The E Editor has two ways to save a file:

- You can save the file periodically and continue editing (press **F2**).

- You can save the file and exit the E Editor (press **F4**).

No matter which method of saving you use, notice that when you begin to save the file, a message appears briefly on the Reminder line, telling you that the file is being saved.

To save the file and continue editing, choose **F**ile, **S**ave or press **F2**. The file is saved in the current directory or in the directory specified with the file name. You can continue editing the file.

To save the file and exit the E Editor, choose **F**ile, **F**ile or press **F4**. The file is saved with its current name and path, and you are returned to Windows or the PC DOS command prompt.

You also can save the file with a new name or in a new directory. Choose **F**ile, Save **A**s, and type the new path and file name on the command line. The file will be saved in the new directory or with the new name.

If you have problems...

If a `File not found` error message is displayed in the function key reminder area when you try to save a file, the file does not yet have a name. A file must have a name before it can be saved. Press **F7** to name the file, and then try saving it again.

Printing a File

You can use the E Editor to print the open file displayed on-screen. Before trying to print a file, make sure that your printer is turned on, that it is loaded with paper, and that it is attached correctly to your computer.

To print a file with the E Editor, follow these steps:

1. Start the E Editor, and open the file you want to print.

2. Choose **F**ile, **P**rint or press **F5**. The E Editor prints the file.

Note: *You can print only a marked portion of a file. Simply mark the text you want to print; choose **E**dit, **P**rint Marked Area; or press **Esc** and type **PRINT** on the command line. When you press **Enter**, the E Editor prints only the marked text.*

The E Editor checks the printer before it prints.

If you have problems...   If the printer is not turned on, is out of paper, or is off-line, the E Editor displays the error message `Printer not ready`. Check your printer, and issue the PRINT command again.

Exiting the E Editor

When you have finished creating or editing text files, you can exit the E Editor and return to Windows or the PC DOS command prompt. You can exit in one of two ways:

■ Choose **F**ile, E**x**it or press **F3** to exit. If you have made changes to any open file since the last time you saved it, the E Editor displays a message in the function key area, asking whether you want to exit without saving. Press **Y** to return to Windows or the PC DOS command prompt without saving the changes. Press **N** to return to the current file.

■ Choose **F**ile, **F**ile or press **F4** if you have more than one file open. The E Editor saves each open file in turn. When all files are closed, you are returned to Windows or the PC DOS command prompt.

7

Chapter 8

Configuring Your Personal Computer

You can configure your computer so that PC DOS, your hardware, and your application programs work the way you need them to in your particular computing environment. This procedure can be as simple as customizing the appearance of the PC DOS command prompt or as complex as setting up a new hardware component.

Memory
The electronic circuitry where the computer stores information.

In addition, you can optimize the way your computer uses available *memory*. By allocating memory resources, you can be sure that your software and hardware run the way you need them to run.

In this chapter, you learn how to use the CONFIG.SYS and AUTOEXEC.BAT files to configure your computer and how to use RAMBoost to make as much memory as possible available for use.

Before you begin to examine and work with the CONFIG.SYS and AUTOEXEC.BAT files and with RAMBoost, you need to understand your computer's memory.

Understanding Memory

On your computer, memory provides temporary storage for programs and data. Your computer has two types of memory: read-only memory (ROM) and random-access memory (RAM).

ROM

Read-only memory that cannot be erased or added to. ROM provides the instructions the computer and PC DOS need to get started.

RAM

Random-access memory—the electronic memory that the computer uses to store information until it is needed or is stored on disk.

Address space

The amount of RAM available for use.

Real mode

The usual mode of operation, where all processors run as fast as 8086-based computers.

Conventional memory

The first 640K of memory installed on every computer. It is used for running the operating system and application programs and for storing data.

ROM is memory that you cannot erase or write on. ROM provides the instructions that the computer needs to get started each time you turn it on. The amount of ROM is determined by the hardware manufacturer. You cannot add more ROM.

RAM is like a blackboard; data constantly is being written, erased, and written again in RAM. Computers come with different amounts of RAM, and you can add more RAM.

RAM is contained on the main system board of your computer or on add-in memory boards. All programs must be loaded into RAM to run. In general, the more RAM you have, the more programs you can run, the more data you can work with at one time, and the faster your computer processes instructions.

Computers that are based on 80286 or higher processors and run the PC DOS operating system have a 1,024K (1 megabyte) *address space* when operating in *real mode*. This figure means that potentially 1M of memory is available.

However, no matter which processor your computer uses or how much memory you have installed, all information is processed in the first 640K—called *conventional memory*. The memory above 640K is reserved for use by devices and other system components.

Many programs have too many instructions to fit into 640K at one time. Waiting for the instructions to be swapped back and forth from a disk to memory is not practical, so computer technicians designed a method to enable your computer to use memory beyond the 640K limit for temporarily storing information.

The types of memory used by computers fall into five categories:

- Conventional memory
- Upper (or reserved) memory
- High memory
- Extended memory
- Expanded memory

Conventional PC DOS Memory

The first 640K of memory installed on your computer is called conventional PC DOS memory. This is the memory that PC DOS uses to process application programs.

Upper (Reserved) Memory

Memory between 640K and 1M is known as the Upper Memory Block (UMB) and is reserved for use by video adapters, network hardware, ROM BIOS, and other hardware that uses computer memory. This memory, however, is never completely used. Some is always left over and can be used for loading TSRs, PC DOS tables, and network software. These Upper Memory Blocks are used by RAMBoost to free conventional PC DOS memory.

High Memory Area

The high memory area is the first 64K of extended memory located just above 1M. Some PC DOS programs running on 80286-based or higher computers can store portions of their operating code software in high memory.

Extended Memory (XMS)

Extended memory is all memory over 1M. Because extended memory cannot be accessed when the processor is in real mode, standard programs running under PC DOS cannot use extended memory.

Protected mode
A special mode of operation that 80286-based or higher computers can use to access extended memory.

On 80286-based and higher machines, some programs, such as RAM disks and disk-caching programs, automatically switch the processor to *protected mode* so that they can access this space. Extended memory can never be used on 8088-based and 8086-based machines, because these processors do not support protected mode or memory above 1M.

Expanded Memory (EMS)

Expanded memory is a combination of hardware and software that uses a 64K area of memory, typically in the address space between 640K and 1,024K. Application programs must be written specifically to switch blocks of memory in and out of this window. The programs themselves use conventional memory to function and access this expanded memory only to store data.

8

Understanding CONFIG.SYS and AUTOEXEC.BAT

Most of your system's configuration information is stored in the two files that PC DOS runs each time you start your computer:

- *CONFIG.SYS*. A file created during installation of PC DOS and stored in the root directory. CONFIG.SYS contains special commands used by PC DOS to control the way the computer, the application programs, and the peripheral devices work. The commands in the CONFIG.SYS set up parameters for your computer's hardware components (such as a memory board, keyboard, mouse, and printer) so that PC DOS and application programs can use them. When PC DOS starts, it processes the commands in the CONFIG.SYS file.

Batch file

A file that contains a series of commands that PC DOS carries out sequentially.

- *AUTOEXEC.BAT*. A special *batch file* created during installation of PC DOS and stored in the root directory. AUTOEXEC.BAT contains a series of commands that PC DOS carries out sequentially immediately after executing the commands in the CONFIG.SYS file. AUTOEXEC.BAT can contain any commands you want to carry out when you start your system. This file can contain commands that define the port to which your printer is connected, clear your screen of start-up messages, or start your favorite application program, for example.

When you install PC DOS, Setup creates a basic system configuration that works for most people. The settings in your CONFIG.SYS file control the basic components of your system, such as memory and disk drives.

You can change your configuration at any time. If, however, you change your CONFIG.SYS file and the new settings are incorrect, your system will not start correctly.

If you have problems...

If you cannot start your computer after you have modified your CONFIG.SYS file, restart your computer using your start-up diskette (Diskette 1 of the PC DOS Setup diskettes), or bypass CONFIG.SYS and AUTOEXEC.BAT commands by using the procedure explained in the following section.

Bypassing CONFIG.SYS and AUTOEXEC.BAT Commands

If necessary, you can start your system without running all or part of your CONFIG.SYS and AUTOEXEC.BAT files. Bypassing these commands is useful if you are experiencing system problems that are related to the settings in your CONFIG.SYS file or AUTOEXEC.BAT file.

You can bypass start-up commands in either of two ways:

- You can bypass your start-up files completely.

- You can have PC DOS confirm each CONFIG.SYS and AUTOEXEC.BAT command when you start your computer.

Bypassing Your Start-Up Files Completely

If you are having system problems that are related to the commands in your CONFIG.SYS or AUTOEXEC.BAT files, you temporarily can bypass those files to start your computer. Then you can make changes to the files to fix the problems.

To bypass the start-up files, follow these steps:

1. Start your computer. Your computer runs through its start-up routine and looks for the PC DOS files. Then the computer displays the message `Starting PC DOS`.

2. Press **F5** as soon as the `Starting PC DOS` message appears. PC DOS skips the CONFIG.SYS and AUTOEXEC.BAT files and loads using a temporary default configuration. The PC DOS command prompt appears on-screen.

If you have problems... Don't worry if your computer does not seem to be working the way it usually does. When you bypass the AUTOEXEC.BAT and CONFIG.SYS files completely, many components of your computer do not work. Any device that requires a software program called an installable device driver, for example, does not work because the installable device drivers are loaded by the commands in the CONFIG.SYS and AUTOEXEC.BAT files.

8

Confirming Each CONFIG.SYS and AUTOEXEC.BAT Statement

Statement

A single command line in a file.

You can have PC DOS prompt you for confirmation before running each *statement* in your CONFIG.SYS and AUTOEXEC.BAT files. This technique is useful if you want to test the commands as they start.

To set PC DOS to request confirmation before carrying out each CONFIG.SYS and AUTOEXEC.BAT command, follow these steps:

1. Start your computer. Your computer runs through its start-up routine and looks for the PC DOS files. Then the computer displays the message `Starting PC DOS`.

2. Press **F8** as soon as the `Starting PC DOS` message appears. PC DOS displays each command in your CONFIG.SYS file, pausing to wait for confirmation.

3. To run the command, press **Y**. To skip the command, press **N**.

4. When PC DOS finishes processing the CONFIG.SYS file, it displays the following prompt:

   `Process AUTOEXEC.BAT [Y,N]?`

5. To confirm each statement in your AUTOEXEC.BAT file, press **Y**. To bypass your AUTOEXEC.BAT file completely, press **N**.

Viewing and Editing CONFIG.SYS or AUTOEXEC.BAT

You easily can view the contents of your CONFIG.SYS file or AUTOEXEC.BAT file by using the PC DOS TYPE command.

To display your CONFIG.SYS file on-screen, follow these steps:

1. At the PC DOS command prompt, type

   TYPE CONFIG.SYS

2. Press **Enter**. PC DOS displays your CONFIG.SYS file on-screen.

To display your AUTOEXEC.BAT file on-screen, follow these steps:

1. At the PC DOS command prompt, type

   TYPE AUTOEXEC.BAT

2. Press **Enter**. PC DOS displays your AUTOEXEC.BAT file on-screen.

Note: *If the file takes up more than one screen, you may need to use the MORE command. At the PC DOS command prompt, type* **TYPE CONFIG.SYS | MORE** *(or TYPE* **AUTOEXEC.BAT | MORE**), *and then press* **Enter**.

Enter the TYPE command

You can view your
CONFIG.SYS file
without affecting
it by using the
PC DOS TYPE
command.

Contents of the
CONFIG.SYS file

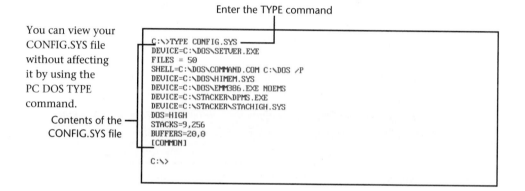

```
C:\>TYPE CONFIG.SYS
DEVICE=C:\DOS\SETVER.EXE
FILES = 50
SHELL=C:\DOS\COMMAND.COM C:\DOS /P
DEVICE=C:\DOS\HIMEM.SYS
DEVICE=C:\DOS\EMM386.EXE NOEMS
DEVICE=C:\STACKER\DPMS.EXE
DEVICE=C:\STACKER\STACHIGH.SYS
DOS=HIGH
STACKS=9,256
BUFFERS=20,0
[COMMON]

C:\>
```

You edit the CONFIG.SYS file or AUTOEXEC.BAT file by using a text editor, such as the E Editor, that can save files as unformatted (ASCII) text. Do not edit these files using a word processing program that saves files in a document format. If you do, PC DOS will not be able to read these files, and your computer will not start. If you have a word processing program that can save files in ASCII format, you can use it to edit CONFIG.SYS. For information on using the E Editor, see Chapter 7, "Working with the Text Editor."

To edit your CONFIG.SYS file or AUTOEXEC.BAT file, follow these steps:

1. Make a copy of the file on a separate diskette or on your hard disk. Name the copied file with a different extension, such as CONFIG.BAK or AUTOEXEC.ARC. If something goes wrong with the edits, you can use the COPY command to copy the original file back into your root directory.

8

2. Open the file you want to edit using the E Editor.

3. Add or change commands as necessary. For information about specific CONFIG.SYS statements or commands, see the following sections.

   Note: *Each CONFIG.SYS or AUTOEXEC.BAT command must begin on a separate line.*

4. When you have finished editing the file, save your changes and exit the E Editor.

5. Restart your system. PC DOS reads the new CONFIG.SYS file and starts your computer accordingly; it then processes the commands in the AUTOEXEC.BAT file.

Note: *Most CONFIG.SYS commands can appear in the CONFIG.SYS file in any order. The PC DOS FILES and BUFFERS commands can appear anywhere in the file, for example. Only the relative order of the DEVICE and DEVICEHIGH commands is important, as discussed later in this chapter.*

If you have problems...

If you change your CONFIG.SYS file and none of the changes makes a difference in the way your system runs, you need to reboot. PC DOS reads the CONFIG.SYS file only when you start your computer. The changes do not affect the way your computer works until the next time you start up. Press **Ctrl+Alt+Del** to reboot your computer and start using the new CONFIG.SYS commands.

Using and Customizing Your CONFIG.SYS and AUTOEXEC.BAT Files

Every computer system has different start-up files. You can customize the way your computer runs by taking time to make sure your start-up files are right for your computer system.

Sample CONFIG.SYS Files

CONFIG.SYS file

The types of devices you have, the amount of memory you have, the way you like to use your computer—all these factors contribute to the way your CONFIG.SYS file looks. In this section, you look at some sample CONFIG.SYS files.

The order in which most commands appear in the *CONFIG.SYS file* does not matter. The order is important for the DEVICE and DEVICEHIGH commands, however. (DEVICEHIGH loads drivers into upper memory.) Some *device drivers* must be in place in order for other device drivers to work.

When adding DEVICE drivers to your CONFIG.SYS file, make sure that they appear in the following order:

- HIMEM.SYS, if your system has extended memory

- Your expanded-memory manager, if your system has an expanded-memory board

- EMM386.EXE, if your system is an 80386 or higher processor with extended memory

  Note: *If your CONFIG.SYS file includes both an expanded-memory manager and EMM386, the EMM386 command line should include the NOEMS switch.*

- DPMS.EXE (DOS Protect Mode Services)

- Any other device drivers

Note: *This list is intended to show the correct order for device drivers, not the specific commands your CONFIG.SYS file should contain.*

The contents of your system's CONFIG.SYS file depend on the type of system, the amount or type of memory, the hardware configuration, and the application programs you use. Some sample CONFIG.SYS files follow.

Device

A hardware peripheral attached to your computer and controlled by PC DOS.

Device driver

A special program file that provides instructions for controlling a hardware device.

A typical CONFIG.SYS file for an 80386 computer with 2M or more of extended memory.

```
C:\>TYPE CONFIG.SYS
DEVICE=C:\DOS\HIMEM.SYS
DOS=HIGH,UMB
DEVICE=C:\DOS\EMM386.EXE RAM
FILES=40
BUFFERS=20
BREAK=ON
DEVICEHIGH=C:\DOS\ANSI.SYS

C:\>
```

8

In this example, note the following points:

■ The DEVICE commands load the HIMEM.SYS and EMM386.EXE device drivers. The HIMEM.SYS driver manages extended memory. The EMM386.EXE driver, when used in a DEVICE= statement with the RAM switch, provides access to the upper memory area and simulates expanded memory.

■ The DOS=HIGH,UMB command runs PC DOS in the high memory area and specifies that programs should have access to the upper memory area. For more information about the upper memory area, see the section "Making More Memory Available," later in this chapter.

■ The FILES command reserves enough room to have 40 files open at one time.

■ The BUFFERS command reserves 20 buffers for transferring information to and from disk drives.

■ The BREAK command checks frequently for the Ctrl+C or Ctrl+Break key combination.

■ The DEVICEHIGH command loads a device driver into the upper memory area.

If you use a network and your system includes an 80286 processor and expanded memory, your CONFIG.SYS file may look like this.

```
C:\>TYPE CONFIG.SYS
DEVICE=C:\EMSDRV\MSDRV.SYS
DEVICEHIGH=C:\DOS\HIMEM.SYS
DEVICE=C:\NET\NETWORK.SYS
DEVICE=C:\DOS\RAMDRIVE.SYS /A
FILES=30
BUFFERS=20
BREAK=ON
LASTDRIVE=Z


C:\>
```

In this example, note the following points:

■ This CONFIG.SYS file loads device drivers for the expanded memory board, the HIMEM.SYS memory manager, and the network.

■ The RAMDRIVE.SYS driver creates a RAM drive in expanded memory.

■ The LASTDRIVE command reserves space for 26 logical drives so that letters from A through Z are available as names for drives.

Note: *You can use a single CONFIG.SYS file to set several different system configurations. This capability can be useful if several people share a single computer or if you want to be able to start your computer with a choice of configurations. For information on defining a CONFIG.SYS file for multiple configurations, see the section "Using Multiple System Configurations," later in this chapter.*

Customizing AUTOEXEC.BAT

Each time you start your system, PC DOS carries out the commands in your AUTOEXEC.BAT file, which is located in the root directory of your hard disk (usually drive C). You can run AUTOEXEC.BAT the same way you run any batch file without restarting your computer. To run AUTOEXEC.BAT from the PC DOS command prompt, type **AUTOEXEC** and press **Enter**.

The commands in the AUTOEXEC.BAT file set the characteristics of your devices, customize information that PC DOS displays, and start *memory-resident programs* and other application programs.

Every command in an AUTOEXEC.BAT file also can be used in other batch programs or issued directly from the PC DOS command prompt. Usually, AUTOEXEC.BAT files are used to run start-up commands, launch memory-resident programs, and change *screen attributes*.

For more specific information about these commands, type **HELP** followed by the command name at the PC DOS command prompt for an explanation and the command syntax.

Start-Up Commands

Table 8.1 describes some of the most common start-up commands used in AUTOEXEC.BAT files.

Memory-resident program

A software program, often a utility, that is stored in RAM as long as it is open for use. Sometimes called terminate and stay resident (TSR).

Screen attributes

The way information is displayed on-screen, including colors, typeface, and character enhancements such as boldface and italics.

8

Table 8.1 Common AUTOEXEC.BAT Commands	
Command	**Purpose**
PROMPT	Sets the appearance of the PC DOS command prompt.
MODE	Sets the characteristics of the keyboard, display, and serial and parallel ports.
PATH	Specifies the directories in which PC DOS searches for executable files (files with a COM, EXE, or BAT file name extension).
ECHO OFF	Directs PC DOS not to display the commands in the AUTOEXEC.BAT file as they run. You also can prevent a command from being displayed by inserting an "at sign" (@) at the beginning of that line.
SET	Creates an environment variable that can be used by programs. The SET command also can be used in the CONFIG.SYS file.
CLS	Clears the screen of all information except the PC DOS command prompt.

Memory-Resident Programs

Another common use of the AUTOEXEC.BAT file is to start memory-resident, or TSR (terminate-and-stay-resident) programs—programs that load into memory and stay there while you use other programs.

PC DOS comes with several memory-resident programs that commonly are started from the AUTOEXEC.BAT file, including the following:

APPEND	FASTOPEN
CPSCHED	KEYB
DATAMON SENTRY (or TRACKER)	MOUSE
DOSKEY	SMARTDRV

Screen Attributes

ANSI set graphics mode access sequence
A command statement that defines standard screen display settings.

You can change your screen attributes by using the PROMPT command and an *ANSI set graphics mode access sequence* in your AUTOEXEC.BAT file.

Note: *The ANSI.SYS driver must be loaded in your CONFIG.SYS file if you plan to use an ANSI set graphics mode access sequence in your AUTOEXEC.BAT file.*

There are three kinds of screen attributes:

- *Text format.* Specifies whether text is bold, underscored, blinking, or hidden.

- *Text color.* Specifies the text color.

- *Background color.* Specifies the screen color.

To change screen attributes, follow these steps:

1. Open the AUTOEXEC.BAT file using the E Editor.

Note: *You can have two prompt commands in the AUTOEXEC.BAT file—one to control the information displayed in the PC DOS command prompt and one to control the screen attributes.*

2. On a separate line, type the following PROMPT command:

PROMPT $E[*x;xx;xx*M

In this command syntax,

$E indicates the ANSI access code

x indicates the number that controls the text format

xx indicates the number that controls the text color

*xx*M indicates the numbers that control the screen color, followed by the number that indicates the ANSI set graphics mode

The order in which you type the parameters is not important. However, the parameters must be separated by semicolons.

To identify the text format (*x*), use one of the following options:

1   Changes the text to bold, or high intensity.

4   Changes the text to underscored. This option works on monochrome displays only.

5   Changes the text so that it blinks.

8

7   Changes the screen display to reverse video. Reverse video reverses the foreground and background colors or shades used on-screen. For example, if your screen normally displays dark letters on a light background, reverse video displays light letters against a dark background.

8   Hides the text unless you subsequently change the background color.

To identify the text color (*xx*), use one of the following options:

30   Black

31   Red

32   Green

33   Yellow

34   Blue

35   Magenta

36   Cyan

37   White

To identify the background color (*xx*M), use one of the following:

40   Black

41   Red

42   Green

43   Yellow

44   Blue

45   Magenta

46   Cyan

47   White

If you have problems...

If nothing happens to your screen display after you enter the PROMPT statement and reboot your system, you probably entered a parameter that your computer system does not support. The system ignores the statement, and no change takes place.

This AUTOEXEC.BAT file includes commands to show yellow text on a red background in bold or high intensity.

The PROMPT command that controls the contents of the PC DOS command prompt

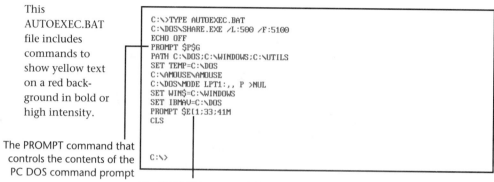

```
C:\>TYPE AUTOEXEC.BAT
C:\DOS\SHARE.EXE /L:500 /F:5100
ECHO OFF
PROMPT $P$G
PATH C:\DOS;C:\WINDOWS;C:\UTILS
SET TEMP=C:\DOS
C:\AMOUSE\AMOUSE
C:\DOS\MODE LPT1:,, P >NUL
SET WIN$=C:\WINDOWS
SET IBMAV=C:\DOS
PROMPT $E[1;33;41M
CLS


C:\>
```

The PROMPT command that controls screen attributes

Sample AUTOEXEC.BAT Files

Every computer system has a different AUTOEXEC.BAT file. The memory-resident programs you have, the start-up commands you want to use, and the way you like to use your computer—all these factors contribute to the way your AUTOEXEC.BAT file looks. This section presents two sample AUTOEXEC.BAT files.

This simple AUTOEXEC.BAT file contains some of the most commonly used commands.

```
C:\>TYPE AUTOEXEC.BAT

PATH C:\DOS;C:\WINDOWS;C:\UTILS
PROMPT $P$G
SET TEMP=C:\DOS
DOSKEY
C:\DOS\SMARTDRV.EXE
CLS


C:\>
```

8

In the preceding example, note the following points:

■ The PATH command directs PC DOS to search for program files in the current directory and then in the following directories: the root directory of drive C, C:\DOS, C:\WINDOWS, and C:\UTILS. A semicolon (;) sets off each directory.

■ The PROMPT command sets the command prompt so that it shows the current drive and directory followed by a greater than sign (>).

■ The SET command creates an environment variable named TEMP and sets it equal to the directory C:\DOS.

Note: *When you set a temporary environment, the name you specify must be the name of an existing directory.*

■ The DOSKEY command loads the DOSKey program into memory. DOSKEY.COM can be located in any directory listed in the PATH command.

■ The SMARTDRV command loads the SMARTDrive program into memory.

A typical AUTOEXEC.BAT file for a system with one diskette drive, one hard disk drive, a laser printer connected to port COM1, and Windows.

```
C:\>TYPE AUTOEXEC.BAT
@ECHO OFF
PATH C:\DOS;C:\WINDOWS;C:\UTILS
PROMPT $P$G
MODE LPT1=COM1
SET TEMP=C:\DOS
DOSKEY
C:\DOS\SMARTDRV.EXE
WIN


C:\>
```

In the preceding example, note the following points:

■ The ECHO OFF command prevents the AUTOEXEC.BAT commands from being displayed as they are carried out. The @ sign at the beginning of the line prevents the ECHO OFF command itself from being displayed.

■ The MODE command redirects printer output from LPT1 (its default port) to the serial port COM1.

- The DOSKEY command loads the DOSKey program, which provides keyboard shortcuts at the PC DOS command prompt.

- The WIN command starts Windows.

Using Multiple System Configurations

You can use a single CONFIG.SYS file to set several different system configurations. This capability can be useful if several people share a single computer or if you want to be able to start your computer with a choice of configurations.

Defining multiple configuration commands can consist of four procedures:

- Defining configuration blocks in your CONFIG.SYS file

- Defining a start-up menu in your CONFIG.SYS file

- Using INCLUDE statements in your CONFIG.SYS file

- Modifying the AUTOEXEC.BAT file

Defining Configuration Blocks

Configuration block
A grouped set of CONFIG.SYS commands used to specify multiple start-up configurations.

A *configuration block* is a grouped set of CONFIG.SYS commands. A configuration block can contain any command you normally put in your CONFIG.SYS file.

To specify a configuration block, you type a *block header*—the block name enclosed by brackets—and then you type the commands you want included in the group, with each command on its own line.

Block header
The name of the configuration block, enclosed in brackets and typed on the first line of the configuration block.

The block name must be a single word, but it can be as long as you want. Some typical block names follow:

- *[MENU]*. Used to define a start-up menu.

- *[COMMON]*. Used to define a block of commands common to all configurations.

INCLUDE is used to define a block that includes a previously defined block.

8

When PC DOS comes to a block in a CONFIG.SYS file, PC DOS carries out all the commands between the block header and the next block header, or the end of the file.

This part of a CONFIG.SYS file defines three configurations and includes several common commands.

```
[CPSW]
COUNTRY=001,,C:\DOS\COUNTRY.SYS
DEVICEHIGH=C:\DOS\DISPLAY.SYS CON=(EGA,,1)
[DLS]
DEVICEHIGH=C:\NET\PROTMAN.DOS /i:C:\NET
DEVICEHIGH=C:\NET\IBMTOK.DOS
[INTLNK]
DEVICEHIGH=C:DOS\INTERLNK.EXE
[COMMON]
DEVICEHIGH=C:DOS\ANSI.SYS
SHELL=C:\DOS\COMMAND.COM /P/E:512
FILES=30
BUFFERS=30
LASTDRIVE=Z
BREAK=ON
DEVICE=C:\DOS\HIMEM.SYS
DOS=HIGH,UMB
DEVICE=C:\DOS\EMM386.EXE NOEMS
DEVICE=C:\DATA\SETVER.EXE
```

This CONFIG.SYS file configures the computer for code page switching and keyboard support [CPSW], LAN networking [DLS], and laptop computer connectivity [INTLNK]. For all three configurations, PC DOS runs the commands in the [COMMON] configuration block.

Defining a Start-Up Menu

At the beginning of the CONFIG.SYS file with multiple configurations, you should define a start-up menu. To do this, create a configuration block with the block heading [MENU]. A menu block can contain any of the following commands:

- *MENUITEM.* Used to define each item on the menu.

- *MENUDEFAULT.* Used to specify the default configuration.

- *MENUCOLOR.* Used to set the text color.

- *SUBMENU.* Used to define submenu items, if necessary.

- *NUMLOCK.* Can be set to On or Off.

When your computer starts, the start-up menu appears and lists the available configurations. You are prompted to choose the configuration you want.

A sample start-up menu is defined for the configurations shown in the preceding section.

```
[MENU]
MENUITEM=DLS, LOAD DOS LAN SERVICES CLIENT
MENUITEM=INTLNK, LOAD INTERLNK CLIENT
MENUITEM=CPSW, LOAD CODE PAGE SWITCHING
MENUCOLOR=7,1
MENUDEFAULT=DLS,20
NUMLOCK=OFF
```

In this example, note the following:

- The MENUITEM command specifies each of three possible configurations. The first MENUITEM command value specifies the configuration block header. The second value, which is optional, specifies the text to display on the menu. If you do not specify any menu text, PC DOS uses the name of the configuration block as the menu text.

- The MENUCOLOR command sets the text color to 7 (white) and the background color to 1 (royal blue).

- The MENUDEFAULT command is optional. It specifies which menu item is to be the default configuration. When PC DOS displays the start-up menu, the default menu item is highlighted, and its number appears after the Enter a choice prompt. If no item is specified, the default is set to the first item.

Timeout value
The amount of time PC DOS waits for the user to select a menu item. If nothing is selected in this time, PC DOS selects the default item.

Note: *With the MENUDEFAULT command, you also can specify a timeout value. You can specify a timeout value from 0 through 90 seconds. If the user does not select an item within the specified time, PC DOS selects the default item. In this example, the timeout value is 20 seconds.*

Using INCLUDE Statements

The CONFIG.SYS file also can contain the INCLUDE command, which enables you to include the contents of one configuration block in another block.

The INCLUDE command instructs PC DOS to carry out the commands in another configuration block, as well as the commands in the current block. INCLUDE can be used only within a configuration block.

8

Suppose that you want to add another configuration that combines all three of the previously discussed configuration blocks. You can use the INCLUDE command to do this by adding a fourth configuration similar to the following:

A fourth user-specified configuration name, called [LOADALL], is defined. It uses the INCLUDE menu command to combine all three of the other configurations.

```
[LOADALL]
INCLUDE=CPSW
INCLUDE=DLS
INCLUDE=INTLNK

[COMMON]
SET PATH=C:\NET\C:\DOS
```

Note: *Placing a [COMMON] block at the end of your CONFIG.SYS file is a good practice, even if the block does not contain any commands. Some application programs append commands to your CONFIG.SYS file. If your CONFIG.SYS file has a [COMMON] block at the end, an application program can append commands to the CONFIG.SYS, and PC DOS will carry out those commands for all your configurations. If you do not want the commands carried out for all your configurations, you should manually enter the commands into the appropriate configuration blocks.*

Modifying the AUTOEXEC.BAT File

When you use multiple configurations, you may want to set PC DOS to run different AUTOEXEC.BAT commands for each configuration. You can create branching code in the AUTOEXEC.BAT file by using batch commands, such as the IF and GOTO commands. With batch commands, you can have PC DOS carry out different AUTOEXEC.BAT commands depending on the start-up configuration.

When the user selects a configuration from the start-up menu, PC DOS sets the CONFIG environment variable to the name of the selected configuration block. In the AUTOEXEC.BAT file, you can use the IF command to test the value of the CONFIG variable and then have PC DOS carry out different commands for different values.

When you test the value of the CONFIG variable, you enclose it in both percent marks (%) and quotation marks ("), as shown in the following example. For information about the IF command, type **HELP IF** at the PC DOS command prompt.

The
AUTOEXEC.BAT
file tests the
CONFIG variable
and runs different
commands,
depending on the
result of the test.

```
C:\>TYPE AUTOEXEC.BAT
@ECHO OFF
PATH C:\DOS;C:\NET
PROMPT $P$G
SET TEMP=C:\DOS

IF "%CONFIG%" == "DLS" C:\NET\NET START

IF NOT "%CONFIG%" == "CPSW" GOTO NOTCPSW
MODE CON CODEPAGE PREPARE=((850)) C:\DOS\ISO.CPI
MODE CON CODEPAGE SELECT=850
LOADHIGH KEYB US

:NOTCPSW
CHOICE /C:YN /TN,3 Do you want to load MOUSE support?
IF ERRORLEVEL 2 GOTO SKIPMOUSE
LOADHIGH C:\DOS\MOUSE.COM

:SKIPMOUSE
LOADHIGH DOSKEY
SETIBMAV=C:\DOS
C:\DOS\
CALL C:\DOS\IBMAVDR.BAT C:\DOS\

C:\>
```

When PC DOS runs this AUTOEXEC.BAT file, it sets the path, command
prompt style, and the TEMP environment variable.

PC DOS then tests the value of the CONFIG variable. The CONFIG.SYS
value was set when you entered your choice of configuration from the
start-up menu.

In the example, if the name of the current configuration is not CPSW,
PC DOS inquires whether you want mouse support. If you do not want
to load the mouse or you do not make a choice within three seconds,
mouse support is not loaded.

Whether or not you choose to have mouse support, this configuration
then runs the DOSKey program and starts IBM AntiVirus/DOS.

Analyzing Your Computer's Memory

Programs that run with PC DOS normally use your system's conventional
memory. Many programs also can use extended or expanded memory if
it is available. If your system has an 80386-based or higher processor, you
also can run programs in the upper memory area. You have two ways
to find out about your computer's memory: the MEM and QCONFIG
commands.

8

The MEM Command

You can use the MEM command to display a status report that details the type of memory your system has, how much memory is in use, and which programs currently are loaded into each type of memory.

To display a MEM status report, type **MEM** at the PC DOS command prompt and press **Enter**.

The MEM command displays a status report of memory configuration and usage.

```
C:\>MEM

Memory Type          Total  =   Used   +   Free
                     ------      ------     ------
Conventional          640K       258K       382K
Upper                   0K         0K         0K
Reserved              384K       384K         0K
Extended (XMS)     15,360K     2,436K    12,924K
                     ------      ------     ------
Total memory       16,384K     3,078K    13,306K

Total under 1Mb       640K       258K       382K

Total Extended (XMS)            15,360K  (15,728,640 bytes)
Free Extended (XMS)             12,924K  (13,234,176 bytes)

Largest executable program size    382K    (391,008 bytes)
Largest free upper memory block      0K          (0 bytes)
The high memory area is available.

C:\>
```

To display a status report that includes a list of programs currently loaded in memory, follow these steps:

1. At the PC DOS command prompt, type **MEM /C/P**.

   The /C switch tells PC DOS to list programs currently loaded in memory. The /P switch tells PC DOS to pause at the bottom of each screen of information.

2. Press **Enter**.

A list of programs
loaded in memory
is included in the
status report.

```
Modules using memory below 1Mb:

Name          Total       =   Conventional    +   Upper Memory

IBMDOS       63,248   (62K)     63,248   (62K)           0   (0K)
SETVER          736    (1K)        736    (1K)           0   (0K)
HIMEM         3,264    (3K)      3,264    (3K)           0   (0K)
EMM386        2,368    (2K)      2,368    (2K)           0   (0K)
STACKER      52,800   (52K)     52,800   (52K)           0   (0K)
COMMAND       4,800    (5K)      4,800    (5K)           0   (0K)
SMARTDRV     28,592   (28K)     28,592   (28K)           0   (0K)
MOUSE        17,776   (17K)     17,776   (17K)           0   (0K)
DOSKEY        3,952    (4K)      3,952    (4K)           0   (0K)
SAVE         80,752   (79K)     80,752   (79K)           0   (0K)
IBMAVSH       5,632    (6K)      5,632    (6K)           0   (0K)
FREE        391,440  (382K)    391,440  (382K)           0   (0K)

Memory summary:

Type of Memory      Total    =      Used     +      Free

Conventional       655,360         263,920         391,440
Upper                    0               0               0
Press any key to continue...
```

The QCONFIG Command

Alternatively, you can use the QCONFIG command to find out what
kind of memory your system has and how much is available for your
application programs. QCONFIG is a utility used to query information
about your computer system. It displays a complete status report,
including information about memory.

To use the QCONFIG command, follow these steps:

  1. At the PC DOS command prompt, type

   QCONFIG /P

   The /P switch instructs PC DOS to pause at the bottom of each
   screen of information.

  2. Press **Enter**. QCONFIG examines your system and displays an
   analysis on-screen.

8

At the bottom of the QCONFIG analysis, you can find information about memory usage.

Device information ─

Memory information ─

```
Pointer Type     : Serial Mouse  Buttons: 3  Int Level: 4
Pointer Version  : 8.01
Equipment        : 1 Parallel Port(s)
                 : 2 Serial Port(s)
                 : 2 Diskette Drive(s)
                 : 1 Fixed Disk(s)
                 : Pointing Device
                 : Math CoProcessor
Serial Port 1    : COM1: 03F8
Serial Port 2    : COM2: 02F8
Parallel Port 1  : LPT1: 0378
Primary Video    : VGA
Diskette Drive A: 3.50"  - 1.44M - 80 Track - Type 4
Diskette Drive B: 5.25"  - 1.2M  - 80 Track - Type 2
Fixed Disk 1     :     249MB (   255,000KB) (  261,120,000 bytes)  Type 47
Logical Drive C  : Size  254,716KB (   248.7MB) Avail  200,984KB (   196.2MB)
Logical Drive D  : Drive not ready
Total Memory     :  16,000KB (15.6MB)
Conventional     :        640KB  Free:      382KB
Extended Memory  :  15,360KB  Free:        0KB
XMS Memory       :  12,924KB  Free:  12,924KB
XMS Version      : 3.0
Adapter ROM 1    : Addr C0000-C7FFF Cirrus Quadtel VIDEO

C:\>
```

You can save the information from the QCONFIG analysis so that you have a description of your current system configuration. You can print the file by using the E Editor. For information on using the E Editor, see Chapter 7, "Working with the Text Editor."

To save the QCONFIG analysis to a file, take one of the following actions:

- At the PC DOS command prompt, type **QCONFIG /O** to direct the information to a file named QCONFIG.OUT.

- At the PC DOS command prompt, type **QCONFIG /O*filename.ext*** to direct the information displayed to a text file of your choice.

If you have problems...

If you try to direct the output to a file of your choice, but PC DOS displays the following message, you left a space between the /O switch and the file name:

```
Argument ignored - 'filename.ext'
```

```
Output redirected to file 'QCONFIG.OUT'
```

Note: *For more information about the QCONFIG command, type **HELP QCONFIQ** at the PC DOS command prompt.*

Making More Memory Available

To run a program, your system must contain as much physical memory as that program requires. Some programs require more memory than others. If you do not have enough memory to run a program, you can take one of two actions:

■ You can increase the amount of physical memory on your system by plugging a memory board into a slot inside your computer.

■ You can adjust your computer's configuration to make more of your existing memory available to programs.

Some programs do not run even if your system does contain sufficient physical memory. The cause is often that memory-resident programs are taking up some memory and not enough memory is left over. Changing your memory configuration can help make memory available by changing the way the computer allocates memory usage.

PC DOS comes with a memory optimizer utility program called RAMBoost. *RAMBoost* automatically adjusts your computer's configuration to make the best possible use of all available memory.

Using RAMBoost

RAMBoost is a memory optimizer utility program that automatically adjusts your memory configuration to optimize memory usage.

When you run the RAMBoost Setup program, it analyzes your current configuration and then makes the necessary adjustments to increase your computer's available conventional memory.

After RAMBoost is installed, it analyzes your computer's existing configuration and automatically reconfigures programs to load into upper memory every time you start your computer.

RAMBoost manages the Upper Memory Block (UMB) of your computer from 640K to 1,024K. RAMBoost runs invisibly on your computer, optimizing available memory automatically each time your computer's system configuration changes.

8

If you add or remove programs from your CONFIG.SYS file or AUTOEXEC.BAT file, RAMBoost automatically detects the change, reboots, and rearranges the remaining drivers in upper memory.

Memory manager
A utility program that makes the open areas in your Upper Memory Blocks available for loading memory-resident programs and device drivers.

RAMBoost works with a *memory manager* to load device drivers and utility programs into upper memory in order to make more conventional memory available for running application programs.

If you are familiar with memory-management techniques, you can customize RAMBoost's performance by manually editing the settings in the RAMBOOST.INI file.

For example, RAMBoost detects software that can cause incompatibilities when loaded into upper or high memory. In some cases, you might gain more conventional memory by manually shifting the position of the memory manager in the CONFIG.SYS file; however, this change generally is not necessary.

Understanding RAMBoost System Requirements

To use RAMBoost Setup, your system must meet the following requirements:

- A minimum of 512K extended memory

- An 80386SX-based, 80486-based, or higher processor

- For Upper Memory Block support, at least 640K and an EEMS/EMS 4.0 memory manager

RAMBoost supports the following EEMS/EMS 4.0 memory managers:

- HIMEM.SYS and EMM386.EXE provided with PC DOS

- Quarterdeck Expanded Memory Manager-386

- Qualitas 386MAX and BlueMAX

- Helix Netroom

Configuring RAMBoost

You configure RAMBoost by running the RAMBoost Setup program.

Before you configure RAMBoost, make the following preparations:

- Make sure that all adapter cards installed on your computer are loaded or activated. If you do not have your adapter activated, RAMBoost Setup will incorrectly use the adapter memory space.

- When you are using QEMM386, 386MAX, or Netroom, you must install it according to its installation instructions and make sure that it provides Upper Memory Blocks.

- Make backup copies of your CONFIG.SYS and AUTOEXEC.BAT files as a precaution.

- Remove all INSTALLHIGH statements from your CONFIG.SYS file.

- Use the MEM command to save information about your memory to an output file so that you can compare it later to see the results you get after you have loaded RAMBoost.

If you have problems...

To save the output of the MEM command, type **MEM /C > *filename.ext*** at the PC DOS command prompt. The MEM command is preferable to QCONFIG in this case because MEM gives more details about your program's upper memory.

To configure RAMBoost, follow these steps:

1. At the PC DOS command prompt, type **RAMSETUP**.

2. Press **Enter**. RAMBoost starts, and a dialog box appears informing you that RAMBoost is about to modify your startup files.

RAMBoost analyzes your system configuration and recommends a course of action. Because each system is different, your system may display a different message than the one shown here.

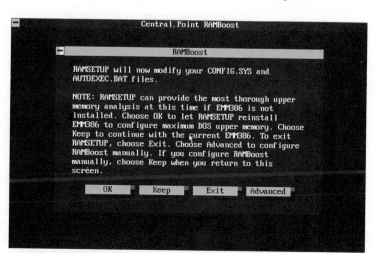

8

3. Depending on your system configuration, follow the instructions that RAMBoost displays on-screen.

   ■ If RAMBoost Setup detects that you have no memory manager installed, choose OK. RAMBoost, EMM386m, and HIMEM are installed into your CONFIG.SYS file.

   ■ If RAMBoost Setup detects that you have installed a memory manager other than the one in DOS, choose OK. RAMBoost is installed into your CONFIG.SYS file.

   ■ If RAMBoost Setup detects that you have an EMM386 statement in your CONFIG.SYS file, choose OK to let RAMBoost comment out the statement and install a new EMM386 statement to optimize your system. Choose Keep to keep your existing EMM386 statement.

   ■ If RAMBoost Setup cannot find a memory manager on your computer, it informs you that you must install one.

   ■ If you have multiple configurations and want to dictate how RAMBoost Setup should handle each one, choose REORGA-NIZE. RAMBoost Setup rearranges the commands in your common section to optimize compatibility with each configuration. The old CONFIG.SYS file is saved as CONFIG.SAV.

4. After RAMBoost Setup installs RAMBoost in your CONFIG.SYS file, the following screen appears.

RAMBoost must reboot your computer in order to analyze your system configurations.

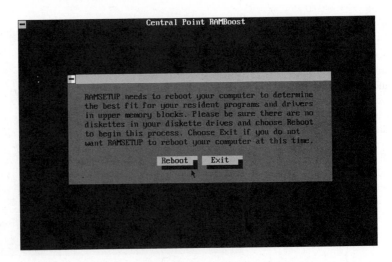

5. Make sure there are no diskettes in drive A or drive B, and then choose Reboot. During this reboot, RAMBoost loads in learn mode and analyzes your current configuration to determine the best usage of upper memory. Do not touch your keyboard or mouse during the reboot.

As you watch your computer screen, you see RAMBoost boot your computer and run the CONFIG.SYS and AUTOEXEC.BAT files. You do not have to take any action. You will see a prompt for loading RAMBoost, but you should not respond to it.

When the reboot is complete, RAMBoost informs you that it now will modify your startup files again.

6. Choose OK to continue and to reboot the computer again.

During the second reboot, RAMBoost actually arranges the programs to fill your computer's upper memory as much as possible, freeing conventional memory. As you watch your computer screen, you will see the message that RAMBoost is loaded in active mode. Finally, the PC DOS command prompt appears. RAMBoost has optimized your memory configuration.

Understanding the RAMBoost Learn Mode

After you run RAMBoost Setup, every time you start your computer, RAMBoost is loaded. If, during start-up, it determines that one of the system files it tracks has been altered, it automatically changes to learn mode.

In learn mode, RAMBoost analyzes the new system configuration to find out whether it needs to change the memory optimization settings. If you watch your computer screen during RAMBoost configuration or during start-up, you see a message indicating that RAMBoost is running in learn mode.

In learn mode, the RAMBoost program is working to determine the optimal location for every object loaded since (and including) the loading of RAMBoost. This process can be long. A feature of the RAMBoost program is a progress bar that shows the current status of the learn function.

8

The progress bar indicates the actual percentage of the possible combinations that have been examined. The time display provides an estimate of how much longer the processing may take. This estimate is based on how long it has taken to process the current fraction of the job.

You can bypass the learn mode at any time. This capability can be useful if you change your AUTOEXEC.BAT and CONFIG.SYS files frequently.

To bypass the learn mode, follow these steps:

1. At the PC DOS command prompt, type **RAMBOOST SYNC**.

2. PC DOS asks for confirmation that you want to bypass the learn mode. Choose **Y**.

Analyzing Your Computer's Memory after Running RAMBoost

After RAMBoost is loaded, you can check to see whether you really do have more conventional memory available.

One way to check that RAMBoost has been successful is to use the TYPE command to display your CONFIG.SYS file.

This line shows DOS is being loaded into high memory

If your CONFIG.SYS file has commands with INCLUDE and EXCLUDE statements and if a RAMBOOST statement appears, you can assume that RAMBoost has been loaded successfully.

This line shows INCLUDE and EXCLUDE statements

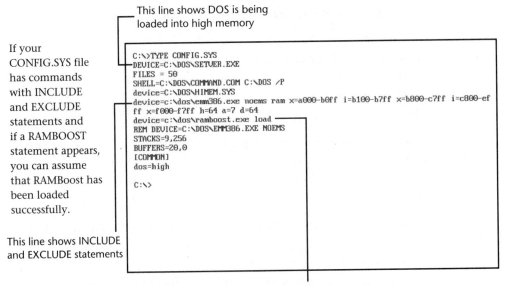

```
C:\>TYPE CONFIG.SYS
DEVICE=C:\DOS\SETVER.EXE
FILES = 50
SHELL=C:\DOS\COMMAND.COM C:\DOS /P
device=C:\DOS\HIMEM.SYS
device=c:\dos\emm386.exe noems ram x=a000-b0ff i=b100-b7ff x=b800-c7ff i=c800-ef
ff x=f000-f7ff h=64 a=7 d=64
device=c:\dos\ramboost.exe load
REM DEVICE=C:\DOS\EMM386.EXE NOEMS
STACKS=9,256
BUFFERS=20,0
[COMMON]
dos=high

C:\>
```

The RAMBOOST statement

Another way to check your memory usage is to use the MEM command to save information about your memory to an output file and compare it to the analysis of memory you made before you loaded RAMBoost. For information on saving the output of the MEM command, see the section "Analyzing Your Computer's Memory," earlier in this chapter.

In the MEM status report, you can see whether RAMBoost has made a difference in the amount of available conventional memory.

Check free conventional memory

```
C:\>MEM

Memory Type          Total  =  Used   +  Free
--------------       -----     ----      ----
Conventional          640K      60K      580K
Upper                 188K      150K      38K
Reserved              196K      196K      0K
Extended (XMS)      15,360K    2,496K   12,864K
                   --------    -----     -----
Total memory        16,384K    2,902K   13,482K

Total under 1Mb       828K      210K      618K

Total Extended (XMS)            15,360K   (15,728,640 bytes)
Free Extended (XMS)             12,864K   (13,172,736 bytes)

Largest executable program size    580K    (594,208 bytes)
Largest free upper memory block     24K     (24,000 bytes)
Available space in High Memory Area  0K        (432 bytes)
PC DOS is resident in the high memory area.

C:\>
```

Using RAMBoost with Other Programs

The following information tells you how to use RAMBoost with specific programs and memory managers.

Helix Netroom386

If you use Helix Netroom386, make sure that the following statement is in your CONFIG.SYS file before you start RAMBoost:

```
device=c:\netroom\rm386.sys ems=c800-efff frame=none
```

Note: *This statement assumes that you are not using EMS.*

Qualitas 386MAX and BlueMAX

If you use Qualitas 386MAX and BlueMAX, the following statement should be in your CONFIG.SYS file before you start RAMBoost:

```
device=c:\max\386max.sys include=b000-b800 ems=512
```

8

If you do not need EMS, change the EMS parameter to read ems=0.
Making this change increases the upper memory available to RAMBoost
by 64K.

If RAMBoost Setup detects 386MAX (Version 7 or later) or detects
BlueMax (Version 6.02 or later), RAMBoost Setup adds the NO58
parameter to the MAX profile. If you install one of these versions
after RAMBoost is loaded, you will need to edit the MAX profile
manually or run RAMBoost Setup again.

Any version of 386MAX or BlueMAX before the version listed should not
include the NO58 parameter in the MAX profile.

RAMBoost Setup deletes from the CONFIG.SYS file two incompatible
BlueMAX or 386MAX (Version 7) devices—both named
EXTRADOS.MAX.

QEMM-386

If QEMM-386 already is installed, you should see the following statement
in your CONFIG.SYS file:

```
device=c:qemm\qemm386.sys ram x=f000-ffff st:m
```

If you do not need EMS, add the NOEMS parameter to this statement in
your CONFIG.SYS file. Making this change increases the upper memory
available to RAMBoost by 64K.

RAMBoost Setup deletes the following incompatible QEMM (Version 7)
devices from the CONFIG.SYS file:

DOS-UP.SYS

DOSDATA.SYS

DESQview and Enhanced Windows

RAMBoost does not automatically reset from the DESQview DOS box or
the enhanced Windows environment. You must reset it manually.

Chapter 9

Controlling the Printer

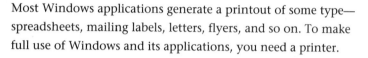

Most Windows applications generate a printout of some type—spreadsheets, mailing labels, letters, flyers, and so on. To make full use of Windows and its applications, you need a printer.

When you install Windows, you choose the printer you want to use with your applications. You can change that printer or select a different printer at any time.

Font
A specific size and style of character that can be displayed on-screen or output to your printer.

In addition to understanding how to use different printers in Windows, you need to understand the different *fonts* that are available. In Chapter 5, "Using File Manager," you learned to change the font used to display the File Manager on-screen. You also can change the fonts used to print.

In this chapter, you learn to use the Windows Print Manager to set up and control the printing of your files. You also learn about using different fonts.

Understanding the Print Manager

The Print Manager comes with Windows and controls printing functions for all Windows applications. Print Manager runs in the background, which means that you can use other applications while files are printing.

You don't actually use the Print Manager to initiate printing. You must issue print commands specific to the Windows application you are using to print the file. To print a file in most Windows applications, choose **F**ile, **P**rint.

9

The Print Manager starts automatically whenever you print a file from a Windows application. When the Print Manager is active, the Print Manager icon appears on the desktop below the application window.

In this figure, the Print Manager icon appears at the lower left corner of the desktop because the Print Manager is active. Sometimes the icon is hidden behind another window.

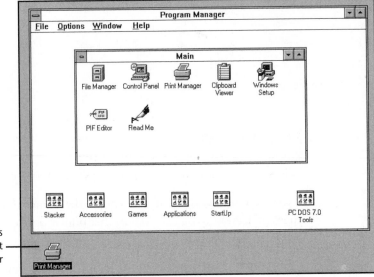

An icon represents the active Print Manager

To open the Print Manager window, take one of the following actions:

■ Double-click the Print Manager icon on the desktop.

■ Double-click the Print Manager icon in the Main group window.

■ Press **Ctrl+Esc** to display the Task List, and then switch to the Print Manager.

If you have problems...   If the Print Manager doesn't start, double-click the Printer icon in the Control Panel window. Make sure that an X is in the Use Print Manager check box.

Click to resume printing

In the Print Manager window, you can control the way your files are printed, and you can change printer setup options.

Click to pause printing

View the file list

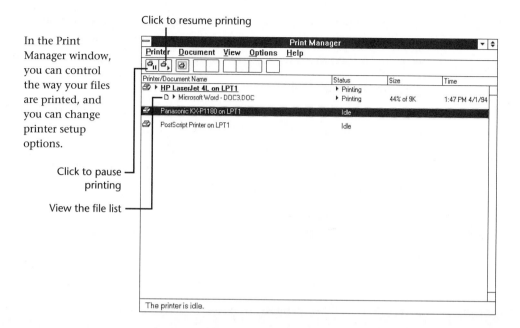

The Print Manager window lists the files waiting to be printed. You can pause the printing, cancel a print job, change the order of files in the print queue, and shift resource priorities between the computer and the printers.

Installing a Printer

Before you can print from Windows, you must install a printer. Usually, you install your printer when you set up Windows. However, you can change printers or install new printers at any time.

Printer driver
A file that gives Windows the printer information it needs to print properly.

Installing a printer in Windows means more than just connecting a printer to your computer. To install a printer in Windows, you must install a *printer driver*, select the *printer port*, and select any special print options you want to use. The following sections provide more details on these tasks. You can have more than one printer installed in Windows at any time, and you can set up the printers with different options. When you want to print a file, you can choose the printer you want to use for that particular print job.

Printer port
The external port on your computer to which your printer is attached.

9

Windows supports many types of printers—dot-matrix, inkjet, and laser, as well as other high-resolution, photo-typesetting printers. Before you install the printer in Windows, read the printer documentation.

Adding Printer Drivers

A printer driver acts like a language interpreter between the computer and your printer. The driver tells Windows such information as the available fonts, printer features, and printer control sequences. Windows comes with many common printer drivers you can use, or you can use a vendor-supplied diskette to load the printer driver into Windows.

Note: *To install a printer driver, you must have a diskette containing the printer driver for Windows. Use your original Windows 3.1 diskettes or the diskette that came from the printer manufacturer.*

To install a printer driver file, follow these steps:

1. Open the Print Manager window.

2. Choose **O**ptions, **P**rinter Setup. The Printers dialog box appears.

In the Printers dialog box, you can add new printers, remove currently installed printers, and change printer setup information.

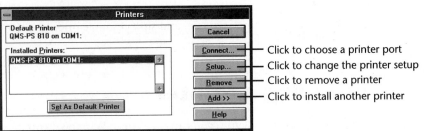

Click to choose a printer port
Click to change the printer setup
Click to remove a printer
Click to install another printer

3. In the Printers dialog box, click **A**dd. The Print Manager displays a list of printers in the lower left corner of the expanded Printers dialog box.

Windows comes
with a list of
printers from
which you can
choose a printer
to install.

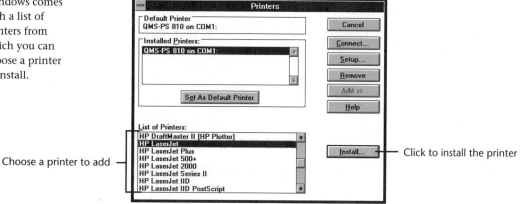

Choose a printer to add ⎯

Click to install the printer

4. From the List of Printers, choose the printer you want.

**If you have
problems...**

If your printer doesn't appear on the list, choose Install Unlisted or Updated
Printer, which appears at the top of the list.

---

5. Click **I**nstall. Windows adds the printer to the list of installed printers and may prompt you to insert a diskette. Continue to follow the
instructions displayed on-screen.

6. Click Close to close the Printers dialog box and return to the Print
Manager window.

Selecting a Printer Port

Printers connect to your computer by means of a cable attached to a
printer port. In order for Windows to print, you need to indicate to
which port your printer is attached. That port can be a parallel (LPT)
or a serial (COM) port. You select the port in the Printers dialog box.

**If you have
problems...**

If you don't know to which port your printer cable is attached, look in your
documentation or ask someone who does know, such as a support techni-
cian or whoever helped you set up your computer.

9

To select a port for your printer, follow these steps:

1. Double-click the Print Manager window.

2. Choose **O**ptions, **P**rinter Setup. The Printers dialog box appears.

3. In the Installed **P**rinters list box, select the printer to which you want to assign a port.

4. Choose **C**onnect. The Connect dialog box appears.

In the Connect dialog box, select the port to which your printer is connected.

Select a port

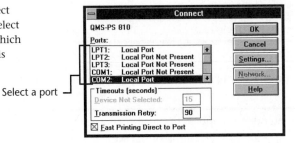

5. Select the correct printer port from the list of ports. Usually, the correct port is identified with the words *Local Port*.

6. Choose OK to return to the Printers dialog box.

Setting Printer Options

You can control the appearance of a document by changing printer setup and printing options.

To view or change your printer settings, follow these steps:

1. Double-click the Print Manager window.

2. Choose **O**ptions, **P**rinter Setup. The Printers dialog box appears.

3. In the Printers dialog box, choose **S**etup. The Setup dialog box appears.

Choose paper options

In the Setup dialog box, you can choose such options as the paper size and orientation.

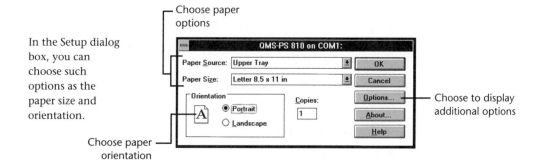

Choose to display additional options

Choose paper orientation

4. Choose the settings you want to change. You can change the paper size, for example, by choosing a different size from the Paper Size drop-down list, and you can enter the number of copies you want to print in the Copies text box. To print the document vertically on the page, choose Portrait in the Orientation area; to print the document horizontally on the page, choose Landscape.

5. Choose Options to display the Options dialog box.

You can set additional printing options in the Options dialog box.

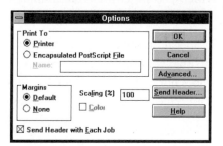

6. Choose the options you want to change.

7. Choose OK to accept the changes and to return to the Setup dialog box.

8. Choose OK to return to the Printers dialog box.

9. Choose Close to close the Printers dialog box.

If you have problems...

Your Setup and Options dialog boxes may look different than the ones used in this chapter, depending on the type of printer you are using. Different printers have different options. For information specific to your printer's printing options, consult your printer documentation.

9

Using Fonts

When you create a document in a Windows application, the appearance of the printed document depends on three factors: the type of printer you have, the fonts available to it, and which fonts you specified in the application.

Understanding Fonts

You can use three basic kinds of fonts with Windows and most Windows applications:

- *Resident* fonts come built into the printer.

- *Font cartridges* can be plugged into some printers to add to their list of resident fonts.

- *Soft fonts* are software files stored on your hard disk.

Scalable
A font that can be made very small or very large without introducing distortions.

In addition to the resident and other printer fonts that come with your printer, Windows comes with a collection of *scalable* soft fonts, called TrueType fonts.

Most fonts appear on-screen almost exactly the way they print, but not all fonts that your printer can print can be displayed on-screen. If Windows does not have a screen font for a printer font, it substitutes a similar font. TrueType fonts print exactly as they look on-screen.

Note: *In Windows applications, you easily can distinguish the printer fonts from the TrueType fonts. In a font list box, the TrueType fonts are indicated with the words* [TrueType] *or a* TT *symbol.*

Adding Fonts

When you install a printer driver, screen fonts are installed automatically along with it. Screen fonts for cartridges and soft fonts usually are supplied on diskette by the vendor. If the vendor doesn't provide an installation program for installing screen fonts, or if you purchase additional TrueType fonts for Windows, you can install the fonts by using the Control Panel Fonts option.

To install a font, follow these steps:

1. Double-click the Control Panel window.

2. Double-click the Fonts icon. The Fonts dialog box appears.

In the Fonts dialog box, you can add and remove fonts and view samples of fonts.

Choose a font ─

A sample of the selected font ─

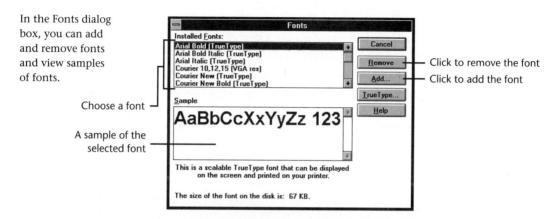

Click to remove the font

Click to add the font

3. Click **A**dd. The Add Fonts dialog box appears.

You can make fonts available for use in Windows in the Add Fonts dialog box.

Choose the fonts to add ─

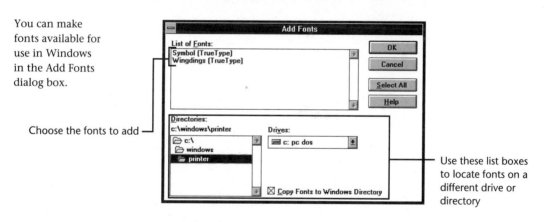

Use these list boxes to locate fonts on a different drive or directory

4. From the **D**irectories and Dri**v**es lists, select the directory and drive that contain the fonts you want to add. If the fonts are on a diskette in drive A, for example, choose A from the Dri**v**es drop-down list.

5. From the List of **F**onts, select the fonts you want to add. To add all the fonts on the list, click **S**elect All.

9

6. Click OK to add the font or fonts. All added fonts appear in the Fonts dialog box.

7. Click Close to close the Fonts dialog box and return to the Control panel.

If you have problems...

TrueType fonts require a great deal of memory. If your computer has a limited amount of available memory and your programs are running slowly or are having trouble loading, you can disable the TrueType fonts. To disable the TrueType fonts, click **T**rueType in the Fonts dialog box and deselect the **E**nable TrueType Fonts check box.

Chapter 10

Using PC DOS 7.0 Tools

There are steps you can take to maintain your system and to keep your software and hardware secure. In this chapter, you learn to protect your system from computer viruses, to defragment your disks, to back up data for safekeeping, and to undelete files that have been deleted accidentally. In addition, you get acquainted with some other tools and features of PC DOS that you can use to optimize the performance of your computer; these tools include PCMCIA support, the MSCDEX command, the REXX programming language, file-update features, and the INTERLNK command.

Protecting Your Computer from Viruses

Virus
A set of computer instructions hidden inside a program that can cause problems ranging from mischievous messages on-screen to the destruction of your programs and data files.

One type of software problem that can harm your disks and cause serious data loss is a *virus*.

Viruses usually are found in free software distributed through electronic bulletin board systems (BBSs) and passed around on diskettes. Operators of bulletin board systems work very hard to avoid viruses, but the risk is not completely eliminated.

To avoid computer viruses, never use a program from someone you do not know. Before you use any program, talk with others who have used the program, and make sure that they have had no problems. Also, make sure that the date and file size of both versions of the program are identical. Having different file sizes on two supposed "copies" of the same program is a clue that the larger file might be infected with a virus.

Another way to help protect your system from viruses is to keep good, up-to-date backups available. Sometimes the only way to clean up an infected system is to restore it, using a virus-free backup. For more information on backing up data, see the section "Backing Up Your Data," later in this chapter.

Viruses are becoming all too common. Fortunately, there are antivirus protection programs you can use to detect and remove viruses from your computer.

PC DOS includes two versions of a powerful antivirus program: IBM AntiVirus/DOS and IBM AntiVirus/Windows. AntiVirus can prevent, detect, and remove computer viruses. The program can work in the background, automatically providing protection at all times, or you can use it to check selected diskettes and hard disks for viruses.

Starting AntiVirus/DOS

To start AntiVirus/DOS, follow these steps:

1. At the PC DOS command prompt, type **IBMAVD**.

2. Press **Enter**. The IBM AntiVirus/DOS screen appears.

AntiVirus/DOS uses a graphical user interface shell. You can use the keyboard or the mouse to make selections from menus or dialog boxes.

Click to scan current drive for viruses

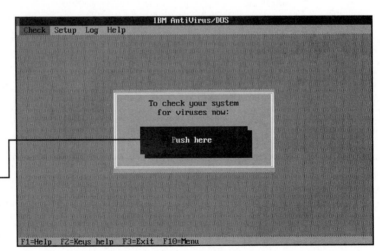

Starting AntiVirus/Windows

To start IBM AntiVirus/Windows, follow these steps:

1. Start Windows.

2. Double-click the PC DOS 7.0 Tools program group window. (For information on opening windows, see Chapter 4, "Making Windows Work."

3. Double-click the IBM AntiVirus icon. The IBM AntiVirus window opens.

The IBM AntiVirus/ Windows program runs in a window like other Windows applications.

Click to scan current disk for viruses

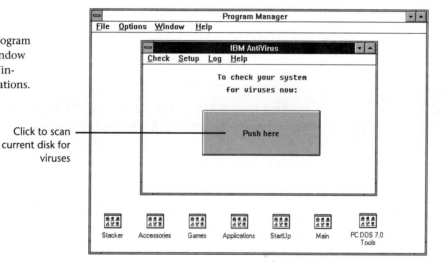

Scanning for Viruses

In either program, follow these steps to scan the current disk for viruses:

1. Start the program as described in the preceding section.

2. Choose Push Here to check the current drive. As AntiVirus scans a disk, it displays a status window telling you that memory is being scanned and showing how many directories and files are being scanned.

3. To interrupt the scan, click the Stop button. A dialog box appears prompting you to confirm that you want to cancel the scan.

4. Choose **Y**es to cancel the scan, or choose **N**o to continue the scan.

When the scan is complete, AntiVirus displays a status report of the viruses found.

Note: *If automated checking detects a virus, you are prompted to perform a thorough examination of your system in order to find every instance of the virus and to remove each one.*

5. Choose OK to return to the main AntiVirus screen.

6. Choose **C**heck, **E**xit to end the program.

The following list includes some of the other functions you can perform with IBM AntiVirus.

■ To check a diskette or diskette drive other than the current drive, choose **C**heck, **C**heck Diskettes.

■ To check your disks for viruses automatically whenever you boot your system, choose **S**etup, **A**utomated Check. You can choose to perform checks at every boot; to perform checks daily, weekly, or monthly; or to perform no checks.

■ To check PC DOS memory for viruses whenever you start PC DOS, choose **S**etup, **Sh**ield DOS. PC DOS Shielding disables viruses and prevents them from becoming active or spreading.

■ To view information AntiVirus gathers during the current scan, choose **L**og, **C**urrent Log.

■ To view the information gathered during the previous scan, choose **L**og, **P**revious Log.

■ To look at all the information gathered during every scan ever performed, choose **L**og, **Cu**mulative Log.

■ To display a list of Help topics, choose **H**elp, **G**eneral Help.

■ To display a list of known viruses, choose **H**elp, Virus **L**ist.

Defragmenting Your Disks

As you add to and delete files from a disk, the space available for new files is spread throughout the surface of the disk. When PC DOS writes a new file to a disk, PC DOS fills the first available space it comes to. If the file requires additional space, PC DOS uses the next available space.

Fragmented
Files that are stored in noncontiguous blocks around the disk.

In this way, files are split apart, or *fragmented*. They are no longer *contiguous*. Fragmented files lower disk performance; to read fragmented files, PC DOS must spend extra time seeking the data among the *noncontiguous* files.

Contiguous
Stored in adjacent blocks on disk.

PC DOS comes with a utility program, PC DOS Defragmenter, that you can use to *defragment* (or optimize) your disks for enhanced performance.

Noncontiguous
Stored in blocks scattered around the disk.

Note: *PC DOS Defragmenter is not found in the PC DOS 7.0 Tools group. You access it from the PC DOS command prompt.*

You can tell how fragmented your disk is by using the CHKDSK command. To check your disk for fragmentation, type **CHKDSK *.*** at the PC DOS command prompt. PC DOS displays a report that shows you the names of noncontiguous files in the current directory. To find all noncontiguous files on the disk, you must repeat the CHKDSK command for every directory.

Defragment
To remove disk fragmentation so that every file on the disk is in its own contiguous block.

Type the command

Use the CHKDSK command to display a status report that includes the number of noncontiguous blocks contained in files on the current disk.

```
C:\>CHKDSK *.*

Volume PC DOS      created 01-04-1995 7:31p
Volume Serial Number is 1D9F-675B

  260,829,184 bytes total disk space
      180,224 bytes in 5 hidden files
       81,920 bytes in 17 directories
   46,354,432 bytes in 1,180 user files
  214,212,608 bytes available on disk

        4,096 bytes in each allocation unit
       63,679 total allocation units on disk
       52,298 available allocation units on disk

      655,360 total bytes memory
      499,392 bytes free

All specified file(s) are contiguous

C:\>
```

Check for noncontiguous blocks

Note: *You cannot defragment a Stacker compressed drive with the PC DOS Defragmenter. You must use the Stacker Optimizer tool found in the Stacker toolbox. For more information, see Chapter 11, "Using Stacker Compression."*

To optimize and defragment your disk, follow these steps:

1. At the PC DOS command prompt, type **DEFRAG**.

2. Press **Enter**. The main defragmenter screen appears.

The Defragmenter uses a graphical user interface. You can use a mouse to select menu items and commands, or you can use a keyboard.

Choose a drive to optimize and defragment

Click OK to continue

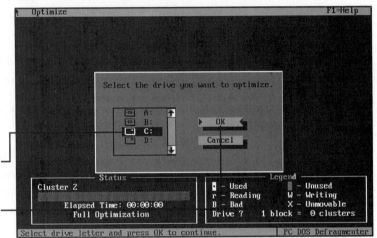

3. Choose the disk drive you want to defragment.

4. Choose OK. The Defragmenter analyzes the disk and makes a recommendation for optimization.

5. Choose Optimize to proceed with the recommended optimization.

Note: *You can choose Configure to select a different method of optimization.*

During optimization, the Defragmenter displays a status screen showing you how blocks of data are being adjusted.

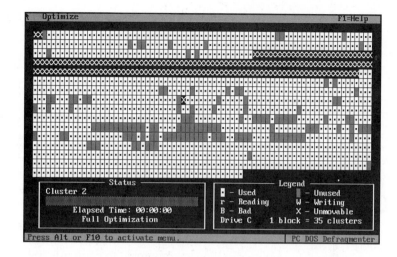

6. Choose OK in the Finished Condensing dialog box that appears when the optimization is complete.

7. Choose another drive to optimize, or choose E**x**it to return to the PC DOS command prompt.

Backing Up Your Data

Back up
To make a copy of your data that can be used in case the original data is accidentally damaged or lost.

If you have ever experienced data loss, you know the value of *backing up* your data. Sudden power failures, software problems, mechanical failures, and user mistakes can lead to the loss of valuable data. An up-to-date backup ensures that you can restore data quickly and resume working.

PC DOS comes with Central Point Backup, a program that provides protection against data loss by enabling you to make a backup copy of data. Central Point Backup can be used from the PC DOS command prompt or from Windows.

With Central Point Backup, you can choose any of the following methods:

■ *Full Backup*. Backs up all selected files.

■ *Incremental Backup*. Backs up all files that have changed since the last full or incremental backup.

- *Differential Backup.* Backs up all files that have changed since the last full backup.

- *Unattended Backup.* Backs up your data to a tape, hard disk, or a network volume at a time you specify.

Central Point Backup also includes utilities for comparing and verifying the backed-up data, and for restoring the backed-up data to its original source location.

Using Central Point Backup

The first time you start Central Point Backup, using either PC DOS or Windows, you are prompted to configure the program for your computer system. Configuring Central Point Backup saves certain information about your system in a Central Point Backup system file. Central Point Backup uses the information to perform reliable backups.

Configuring is automatic. All you have to do is to confirm the type of drives you have, and Central Point Backup does the rest. Simply follow the prompts that appear on-screen throughout the procedure. For more information, use the Help option in the Central Point Backup program.

The first time you run Central Point Backup from Windows, you are prompted to configure it for your system.

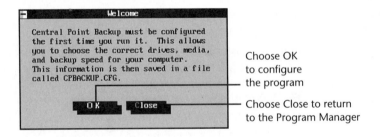

Choose OK to configure the program

Choose Close to return to the Program Manager

Using Central Point Backup for PC DOS

To start Central Point Backup for PC DOS, follow these steps:

1. At the PC DOS command prompt, type **CPBACKUP**.
   The Backup program starts and appears on-screen.

Click to back up your files

Central Point
Backup for PC DOS
uses a GUI. You
can use the mouse
or the keyboard to
choose menu items
and commands.

Click to restore
backed-up files

Click to compare
backed-up files to
original files

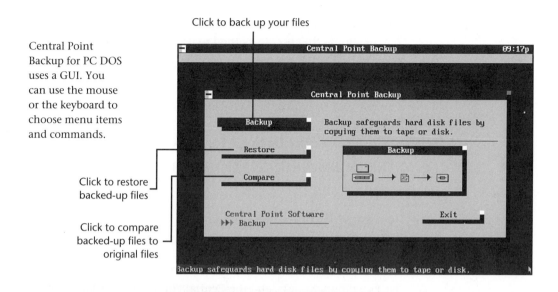

If you have problems...   If you are using Central Point Backup for the first time, the Welcome screen prompts you to configure the program. Choose OK to begin the configuration, and then follow the instructions that appear on-screen.

2. Choose **B**ackup. The Backup screen appears.

For systems with more than one disk
drive, choose the drive to back up from

Click to choose files to back up

From the Central
Point Backup
screen, you can
easily select the
type of backup you
want to perform,
load setup files,
and select the
files you want
to back up.

Click to choose
a setup file

Click to choose
a backup method

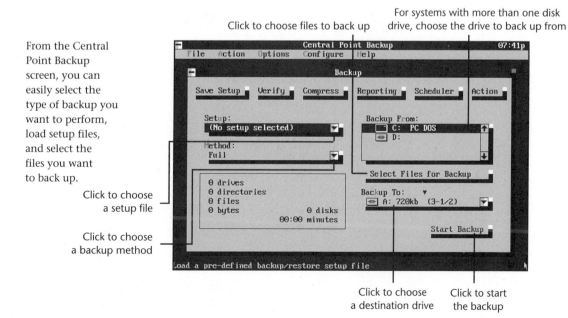

Click to choose   Click to start
a destination drive   the backup

3. Choose the options you want to use for the backup. Choose a setup file; or choose the specific method to use, and select the files you want to back up. For more information, consult on-line Help for this utility.

4. Choose Start Backup to begin backing up.

Using Central Point Backup for Windows

To start Central Point Backup for Windows, follow these steps:

1. Start Windows.

2. Double-click the PC DOS 7.0 Tools group window. For information on opening windows, see Chapter 4, "Making Windows Work."

3. Double-click the Central Point Backup icon. The Central Point Backup program starts, and the Central Point Backup Main Menu window appears on-screen.

If you have problems... If you are using Central Point Backup for the first time, the Welcome screen prompts you to configure the program. Choose OK to begin the configuration, and then follow the instructions that appear on-screen.

From the Central Point Backup Main Menu window, you can choose to back up, restore, or compare data.

Choose **B**ackup

4. Choose **B**ackup to display the Central Point Backup program window.

10

With Central Point Backup, you can easily select the type of backup you want to perform and the files or directories you want to back up.

Click to choose a built-in setup file

For systems with more than one disk drive, choose the drive to back up from

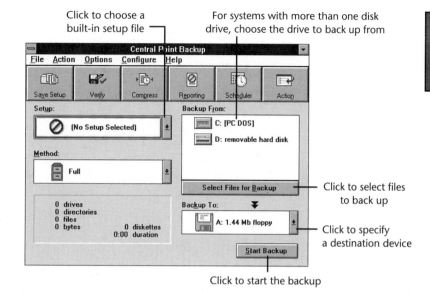

Click to select files to back up

Click to specify a destination device

Click to start the backup

5. Choose the options you want to use for the backup. Choose a setup file; or choose the specific method to use, and select the files you want to back up. For more information, consult on-line Help for this utility.

6. Choose **S**tart Backup to begin backing up.

Understanding Backup Strategies

The key to an effective backup strategy is scheduling. You must determine how frequently you need to back up to ensure a minimal amount of data loss in case of a catastrophe. How often you should back up and the type of backup you should use depend in large part on how frequently your data changes.

Consider the following questions:

- How valuable are my files to me or my business?

- How many of my files change daily?

- How long would it take to replace those files if something happened to them?

With this information, you can determine the backup strategy that best suits your needs.

When you develop a backup strategy, follow these general guidelines:

Backup media
The storage media on which you store the backed up data.

- Alternate between two sets of *backup media* (usually disks or tape, or a combination of the two) so that you are never overwriting your last backup with the current backup.

- Schedule a set time each day for backing up. Schedule weekly backups on Fridays and daily backups on Mondays through Thursdays.

No matter what type of media you use to back up, you can use two of Central Point Backup's built-in setup files to make sure that your backup data always is current.

- The weekly setup file is set to back up all files on your first hard disk (usually C).

- The daily setup file backs up only the changed files since the last full or incremental backup.

Diskette Backup Strategies

To back up all files to diskettes on a weekly basis, follow these steps:

1. At the scheduled weekly backup time on Friday, start Central Point Backup from the PC DOS command prompt by typing **CPBACKUP WEEKLY**.

2. Begin your backup, using the first set of diskettes.

3. Label each diskette with its backup sequence number, name, and set number. For example, label the first diskette "#1, Friday backup, Set A." The next diskette would be "#2, Friday backup, Set A," and so on.

To back up only changed files on a daily basis, follow these steps:

1. At the scheduled backup time, start Central Point Backup from the PC DOS command prompt by typing **CPBACKUP DAILY**.

10

2. Insert the backup diskettes as prompted.

3. Label each diskette with its proper sequence number ("#1 of Set A, Tuesday," "#2 of Set A, Tuesday," and so on).

For many people, a monthly full backup is sufficient when coupled with daily backups of the changed files.

One of the following daily methods should be used, depending on each person's particular needs:

- Do a daily differential backup to diskettes. Alternate between two sets of disks for safety. When the sets use more than six diskettes, do another full backup. The differential method does not save multiple daily versions of the changed files. It saves only the latest versions.

- Do a separate incremental backup on Monday (which starts a new backup set), followed by daily incremental backups to diskettes. This keeps daily versions of the files that change but creates fewer backup sets than using separate incremental backups exclusively.

Tape Backup Strategies

Although your computer system probably did not come with a tape backup system, you may want to consider adding one. A tremendous advantage to using a tape drive is that it automates the backup procedure. One simple strategy is to use at least two tapes so that you are never writing over your latest backup with the current backup. You can use Central Point Backup's built-in weekly and daily setup files to facilitate a two-tape backup strategy.

To back up data using the two-tape strategy, follow these steps:

1. Schedule a weekly full backup, using the WEEKLY setup file and tape #1.

2. Schedule a daily backup using the DAILY setup file and tape #1.

3. Use tape #2 the second week, and continue alternating tapes each week.

Undeleting Files and Directories

PC DOS comes with the Central Point Undelete program (Undelete), which you can use to recover most files and directories that have been deleted using the DELETE command.

Undelete is installed automatically when you install PC DOS. You also can choose to install a version of Undelete for Windows.

Undelete can undelete most files, but it is most effective when you protect files with one of the following methods of deletion protection:

- Delete Sentry

- Delete Tracker

- Novell NetWare 386

- DR DOS DelWatch

Note: *For more information about these deletion-protection methods, see the section "Understanding Deletion-Protection Methods," later in this chapter.*

In any case, you always should undelete files as soon as possible after the deletion to maximize your chances of recovering all your data.

If you have problems...	If you accidentally have erased or formatted your entire disk, use UNFORMAT to recover the disk.

Starting Undelete

Undelete can work with Data Monitor, a memory-resident program that includes several options to guard against data loss and protect important data. You need to add a DATAMON statement to your AUTOEXEC file to have Undelete work with Data Monitor.

You can use Undelete in any of three ways:

- The Windows method enables you to manage your deleted files in the Windows environment.

- The PC DOS command-line method of Undelete is a simplified program that prompts you, file by file, through the files it can undelete.

■ The full-screen PC DOS method uses a graphical user interface to help you locate and recover files.

Starting the Windows Version of Undelete

To start the Windows version of Undelete, follow these steps:

1. Start Windows.

2. Double-click the PC DOS 7.0 Tools group window. (For information on opening windows, see Chapter 4, "Making Windows Work.")

3. Double-click the Undelete icon.

Click to display the contents of a different directory

Click to find a file

Click to sort the file list

In the Windows version of Undelete, you can easily undelete files, display the deleted contents of directories, find files, and sort files—all in the Windows environment.

Click to select a deleted file

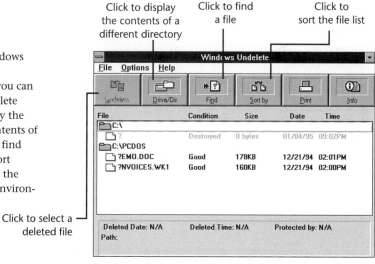

Starting the Command-Line Version of Undelete

To use the command-line version of Undelete, follow these steps:

1. At the PC DOS command prompt, type

UNDELETE *drive:\directory\filename.ext*.

2. Press **Enter**. For each occurrence of a deleted file, PC DOS displays a prompt asking whether you want to recover the file.

3. To recover the file, press **Y**. To leave the file deleted, press **N**.

4. When prompted, enter the first letter of the file name.

Type the command

You can specify
which files you
want to recover
using the
command-line
version of
Undelete.

Respond to
the prompts

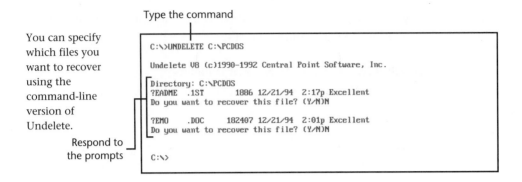

```
C:\>UNDELETE C:\PCDOS

Undelete V8 (c)1990-1992 Central Point Software, Inc.

Directory: C:\PCDOS
?EADME  .1ST      1886 12/21/94  2:17p Excellent
Do you want to recover this file? (Y/N)N

?EMO    .DOC    182407 12/21/94  2:01p Excellent
Do you want to recover this file? (Y/N)N

C:\>
```

You can find out which files have been deleted by using the /LIST
parameter with the UNDELETE command.

To display a list of deleted files with the deletion-protection method
being used, type **UNDELETE /LIST** at the PC DOS command prompt.
PC DOS displays a list of deleted files for the current directory.

Starting the Full-Screen Version of Undelete

The full-screen version of Undelete has a graphical user interface. You
can use a mouse to choose menu items and commands, or you can use
a keyboard.

To start the full-screen version of Undelete, follow these steps:

1. At the PC DOS command prompt, type **UNDELETE**.

2. Press **Enter**. The Undelete program appears on-screen.

You can use a
mouse to choose
commands in
the full-screen
PC DOS version
of Undelete.

Directory Tree area

File List
area

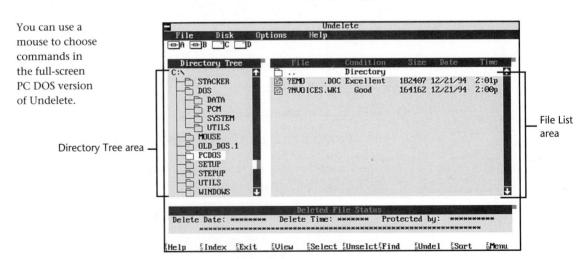

Using the Full-Screen Version of Undelete

When the Undelete window appears, the Directory Tree area on the left shows the directory structure of the selected drive. The File List area on the right shows subdirectories and files that have been deleted from the highlighted directory, as well as any existing subdirectories.

You can use a mouse in Undelete, or you can use function keys. Some of the available function keys are described in table 10.1.

Table 10.1 The Undelete Function Keys

Function Key	Description
F1	Provides on-line Help about the selected item
F2	Displays the Help index
F3	Exits to the PC DOS command prompt
F4	Displays the contents of the highlighted file
F5	Enables you to select files by file name specification
F6	Enables you to deselect files by file name specification
F7	Opens the Find Deleted Files window
F8	Undeletes the selected file or files
F9	Enables you to specify a sort order for listing files
F10	Activates the horizontal menu bar

Understanding the Condition of a Deleted File

Cluster
A unit of disk space where files are stored.

The condition of each deleted file appears next to the file name in the File List area. The condition indicates how completely Undelete can recover the deleted file. Undelete assigns conditions based on the status of the file's *clusters*.

Table 10.2 describes the different file conditions assigned by Undelete.

Table 10.2 The Undelete File Conditions	
Condition	**What You Can Expect to Recover**
Perfect	You can undelete the file completely and automatically.
Excellent	All the file's clusters are available and unfragmented and can be undeleted automatically. There is a slight chance that some data may not be available.
Good	One or more of the file's clusters are in use by another file and are not available. Some data may have been overwritten.
Poor	The file's first cluster and possibly additional clusters are not available. You may be able to use advanced delete methods to recover the data.
Destroyed	The file cannot be undeleted because all its known clusters are in use by other files. You may be able to use advanced delete methods to recover the data.
None	The file cannot be undeleted because it had no data in it when it was deleted.
Existing	The file has not been deleted.
Lost file	The file was found by scanning for lost files. It is a deleted file whose directory probably has been deleted.
Recovered	The file was undeleted during the current session.
Purged	The file was purged from a deletion-protection directory during the current session. It cannot be recovered.

Understanding Deletion-Protection Methods

The Deleted File Status panel indicates what method of deletion protection was being used when the highlighted file was deleted. Table 10.3 describes the different deletion-protection methods.

Table 10.3 Deletion-Protection Methods	
Protection Method	**Description**
Delete Sentry	Files protected by the Delete Sentry method can be undeleted in perfect condition because they are saved in a hidden directory.
Delete Tracker	PC DOS leaves files protected by the Delete Tracker method on the disk but marks the file's clusters as available. As long as the file's clusters have not been overwritten by new data, the file can be recovered in excellent condition.

10

Protection Method	Description
DOS	Indicates that no deletion-protection method was used. Files are undeleted based on their entries in the DOS directory and in the File Allocation Table on the disk.
NetWare	Indicates that Novell NetWare's method of deletion protection was used on a network drive. The files can be undeleted in perfect condition because they actually remain on the drive until they are purged or the space they occupied is overwritten.
DelWatch	Indicates that the DR DOS method of deletion protection was used. Files can be undeleted in perfect condition.

Sorting the File List

By default, Undelete sorts by file name. However, you can change the order in which Undelete displays files by selecting a different sort order. For example, you might want all the BAT files or all the files created on a certain date listed together so that you quickly can find the one you want to undelete. Or if you know that the file is very small, you might sort the list in order of size.

If you select more than one file to undelete, the sort order determines the order in which the files will be undeleted. Before you simultaneously undelete a group of files that have different conditions, sort them in order of condition so that Undelete can recover the files that are in the best condition first. The condition of a file can change as the files preceding it are undeleted.

To change the sort order, follow these steps:

1. Choose **O**ptions, **S**ort By. The Sort by dialog box appears.

In the Sort By dialog box, you can change the sort order to more effectively undelete deleted files.

Choose the sort order ⌐

Choose OK to confirm the change in order

2. Choose one of the following sort orders:

- *Name*. Sorts the files by file name.

- *Extension*. Sorts the files by file extension.

- *Size*. Sorts the files by size, with the smallest files first.

- *Deleted Date and Time*. Sorts files protected by Delete Sentry and Delete Tracker by the date files were deleted. Within each date group, files are sorted in order of time deleted. DOS-deleted files that have an unknown date are listed last in unchanged order.

- *Modified Date and Time*. Sorts the files in order of the date files were last modified. Within each date group, files are sorted in order of time last modified.

- *Directory*. Sorts the files alphabetically by directory name. This option is available only in the expanded file list displayed for network drives and files found by specification, where the directory tree is not shown.

- *Condition*. Sorts the files by condition in the following order: Perfect, Excellent, Good, Poor, Destroyed, Existing.

3. Choose OK.

Selecting Files

You must select the files that you want to undelete. Table 10.4 describes the methods you can use to select files.

Table 10.4 Methods of Selecting Files	
To	**Do This**
Select one file	Use the mouse or the arrow keys to highlight the file you want to select; and click the left mouse button, press **Enter**, or press the **spacebar**.
Select or deselect a group of files with the mouse	Press and hold down the right mouse button. Use the mouse or the arrow keys to highlight the first file you want to select; then press and hold down the left mouse button. Drag the mouse to the last file you want to select. Release both mouse buttons.

To	Do This
Select a group of files by specification	Choose **O**ptions, **S**elect by Name. Enter a file specifcation, and choose OK.
Deselect a group of files by specification	Choose **O**ptions, **U**nselect by Name. Enter a file specification and choose OK.

Undeleting a File

To undelete a file in perfect or excellent condition, follow these steps:

1. Select the file in the File List area.

2. Press **F8**. The file is undeleted and stored in its original directory.

To undelete a file in good condition, follow these steps:

1. Select the file in the File List area.

2. Choose **F**ile, Undelete **T**o. The Drive Selection dialog box appears.

3. Select the disk drive in which to store the recovered file.

4. Choose OK. The Undelete To dialog box appears.

5. Specify a path in which to store the file.

6. Choose OK. Undelete recovers the file.

Note: *Undeleting a file to a different drive is useful as a safety precaution, no matter what condition the deleted file is in. This action leaves the original deleted file unchanged but restores a copy of the file to the specified drive and directory.*

If you have problems...   If the file you want to delete is in any condition other than perfect, excellent, or good, you probably need to use advanced methods to recover the data.

Renaming an Existing File

Existing file
A file that has not been deleted.

If the file you are undeleting has the same name as an *existing file*, Undelete prompts you to change the existing file name. This situation may occur if the deleted file is a previous version of an existing file. You can rename the existing file before you undelete the deleted file and thereby keep both files in the same directory.

To rename an existing file using Undelete, follow these steps:

1. In the Directory Tree area, choose the directory that contains the file you want to rename.

2. Choose **O**ptions, **Sh**ow Existing Files to display existing files in the File List area along with deleted files.

3. In the File List area, select the existing file you want to rename.

4. Choose **F**ile, **A**dvanced Undelete, **R**ename Existing File. The Rename Existing File dialog box appears.

5. Type a new name for the existing file.

6. Choose **R**ename.

Note: *To remove the existing files from the file list, select **O**ptions, **Sh**ow Existing Files again.*

Undeleting Files on a Network

If you are undeleting files on a network drive, Undelete lists the deleted files that were protected by the Delete Sentry or Novell NetWare 386 method of deletion protection. In place of a directory tree, Undelete shows the deleted files' paths in an expanded file list.

If a network directory is hidden, Undelete will not display the files unless the directory's hidden attribute is changed. Also, if you are using Delete Sentry, files deleted by other users do not appear in the list. The Novell NetWare method of deletion protection shows all files; you can undelete files that you have deleted with your current user name.

If you use Novell NetWare's method of deletion protection to protect the network drive, users can see deleted files but cannot recover files unless the network administrator has assigned Create rights to the directory that contained the deleted files.

If none of these methods of deletion protection was used on the network drive, Undelete does not list any deleted files.

The following commands are not available if you are undeleting files on a network drive:

- File, Tree & File List

- File, Advanced Undelete

- All commands on the disk menu

- Options, Show Existing Files

- Options, Use Mirror File

Note: *NetWare does not keep track of deleted directories, but the program does track the files in deleted directories.*

Undeleting Directories and Their Files

A directory contains file entries identifying the names, starting locations, and other information for all files that belong to it. When you delete a directory, deleted files that were in that directory no longer appear in Undelete's file lists. However, the deleted directory appears, identified with a folder icon and <dir> listed as the file size.

As soon as you undelete a directory, any deleted files it contained appear in Undelete's file lists. If you cannot find a deleted file, try to locate its directory by using the Directory Tree and File List area. When you undelete the directory, it appears in the Directory Tree. Select that directory, and then select and undelete any of its deleted files.

If you cannot find a deleted file's directory, you still can find the file or its data by using one of Undelete's disk scan methods. For information on scanning disks for lost files, refer to on-line Help for more information.

To undelete a directory, follow these steps:

1. Select the directory in the Directory Tree area.

2. Press **F8**.

3. If Undelete cannot determine the location of all the parts of the directory, it displays the Directory Undelete dialog box.

In the Directory Undelete dialog box, you must identify the groups of file entries that belong in the directory you are undeleting.

Note: *In the Directory Undelete dialog box, you do not select individual files to undelete. You decide whether the entire group of file entries displayed in the list box represents files that belong in the directory you want to undelete.*

4. In the Directory Undelete dialog box, take one of the following actions:

   ■ If the group of file entries displayed in the File List area was in the directory, select **A**dd.

   ■ If the group of file entries displayed in the File List area was not in the directory, select **S**kip.

5. Undelete searches for the next probable group of files and displays it in the File List area. Repeat step 4 until the entire directory has been recovered.

Note: *Choose Undelete in the Directory Undelete dialog box to recover the directory without selecting all the file groups. Undelete does its best to recover as much of the directory as possible.*

Finding Deleted Files

You can search for deleted files by entering a file specification. This capability is useful if you cannot find a deleted file in the File List area or when you want to display all deleted files on the disk in one listing.

To specify deleted files, follow these steps:

1. Select the drive that contained the deleted file.

2. Choose **F**ile, **F**ind Deleted Files. The Find Deleted Files dialog box appears.

Enter a file specification

You can search a
disk for specified
deleted files.

Enter a text string ——

```
┌─────────────────────────────────────────────────────────┐
│ ─                    Find Deleted Files                  │
│ File Specification:                                      │
│ *.*                                          ┌────────┐  │
│                                              │   OK   │  │
│ Containing:                                  └────────┘  │
│                                              ┌────────┐  │
│                                              │ Cancel │  │
│                                              └────────┘  │
│                                              ┌────────┐  │
│                                              │ Groups │  │
│   ☑  Ignore Case                             └────────┘  │
│   ☐  Whole Word Search                                   │
│                                   ☑   DOS                │
└─────────────────────────────────────────────────────────┘
```

10

3. Complete one or more of the following actions:

- In the File Specification text box, type the file specification for the file or files you want to find. You can use PC DOS wild-card characters.

Text string
A series of text
characters, consist-
ing of words and
numbers.

- In the Containing text box, enter a *text string* that you know is contained in the deleted file you want to find.

- Choose Groups to find files associated with a particular application program.

4. Select one or more of the text search options:

- Choose **I**gnore Case to find files containing the text whether it is uppercase or lowercase.

- Choose **W**hole Word to find the text only if it is entered in complete words.

5. Select the deletion-protection methods for which to search.

**If you have
problems...**

If the Delete Sentry, Delete Tracker, and DelWatch options are dimmed, no files on the current drive are protected by these methods.

---

6. Choose OK. Undelete displays all files that match the specifications in an expanded file list in the Find Deleted Files window.

7. To return to the Directory Tree and File List areas, choose **F**ile, Tree & **F**ile List.

Scanning the Disk for Lost Files and Deleted Data

If you have not found a deleted file by using any of the previous methods, you can scan the entire disk for lost files or for deleted data that is not associated with any file or directory.

To scan the disk for lost deleted files, follow these steps:

1. Select the directory in which you want lost files to be recovered. Undelete recovers lost files to the current directory.

2. Choose **D**isk, Scan for **L**ost Deleted Files. The Scan for Lost Files dialog box appears.

You can scan a disk to try to find deleted files that are no longer associated with a directory.

3. Select the deletion-protection methods for which to scan.

If you have problems...   If no files on the current drive are protected by Delete Sentry or Delete Tracker, that check box is dimmed and you cannot select it.

---

4. Choose OK. Undelete scans the disk for files protected by the method or methods you selected.

When the disk scan is complete, the list of files found appears in the Find Deleted Files dialog box, with Lost File as each file's condition. Lost files retain their original names and other information, so you easily can select and undelete the files you want.

Scanning Free Clusters for Deleted Data

You can scan the disk's free clusters—disk space no longer associated with any existing file or directory—for a specified type of data or a text string.

10

Note: *When scanning the disk's free clusters, Undelete does not look at files protected by Delete Sentry or DelWatch.*

To scan free clusters for deleted data, follow these steps:

1. Select the directory in which you want clusters containing the specified type of data to be recovered. Undelete recovers clusters to the current directory.

2. Choose one of the following:

   ■ *Disk, Scan for **Data** Types.* Selects the type of data to scan for (Lotus 1-2-3 and Symphony, dBASE, or normal text).

   ■ *Disk, Scan for **Contents**.* Specifies a word, phrase, or text string for which to scan. It does not matter whether you use uppercase or lowercase letters.

3. Choose OK.

When Undelete finds a contiguous group of free clusters that match the information you specified, Undelete counts the group as a file and gives it a unique name. Undelete tries to match lost data with directory entries, making its best guess at the file name. When the disk scan is complete, the list of clusters found appears in the Find Deleted Files window.

Using PenDOS

Pen-based
Application programs designed for use with a tablet or digitizer pen input device.

PC DOS comes with PenDOS, a utility program that enables you to use *pen-based* application programs as well as standard mouse-based PC DOS application programs on any 386 or higher computer. Pen-based application programs make computing easier than ever; you can write, draw, and issue commands simply by pointing and using a pen.

PenDOS enables you to use the mouse as a pen. You do not need any other special equipment to compute with a pen.

Tablet
A peripheral device that enables you to input information into a computer by writing on it with a pen device.

Using a pen *tablet* computer or externally attached digitizer tablet, you can write naturally because PenDOS includes CIC's Handwriter Recognition System. As an introduction to computing with a pen, this version of Handwriter recognizes numbers and symbols only. A full version of Handwriter that recognizes uppercase and lowercase letters, numbers, punctuation marks, and symbols is available separately from IBM.

Preparing Your System for PenDOS

You can install PenDOS on your system during PC DOS setup and installation.

Before starting PenDOS, make sure that you have the proper hardware installed and the correct tablet driver selected. If you have a pen tablet computer with a self-contained digitizer, you should have chosen that computer's tablet driver when you set up PC DOS.

If you have an externally attached digitizer, make sure that the digitizer is connected to the proper communication port on your computer. Refer to the digitizer manufacturer's instructions for the proper installation procedure. You also should have selected the proper tablet driver for your digitizer during PC DOS Setup. If you will be using your mouse as your pointing device, select the Digitizing Pad Emulation via Mouse tablet driver during PC DOS Setup.

The PC DOS Setup program modifies your CONFIG.SYS file by adding the appropriate device statement when you select PenDOS as an optional tool and then select a tablet or mouse device.

Starting PenDOS

You can modify your AUTOEXEC.BAT to have PenDOS start automatically whenever you start your computer, or you can type the PENDOS command at the PC DOS command prompt each time you want to start PenDOS.

To start PenDOS, follow these steps:

1. At the PC DOS command prompt, type **PENDOS**.

2. Press **Enter**.

Understanding Phoenix PCMCIA Support

PC DOS provides support for the computers with slots conforming to the Personal Computer Memory Card International Association (PCMCIA) standard.

PC Cards

Credit card-sized devices that attach PCMCIA sockets inside the computer. They are used to attach peripherals such as memory-expansion cards, faxes, and modems.

10

The PCMCIA standard allows for the uniform development of *PC Cards*—credit card-sized devices for portable, laptop, some desktop, and palmtop computer accessories (such as memory-expansion cards, fax and modem attachments, and interfaces to corporate networks). A computer having PCMCIA support provides sockets into which you can insert PC Cards. PC Cards enable you to extend the capabilities of your computer by adding functions, such as the following:

- Communications (modems, Token-Ring, EtherNet, 3270, and 5250)

- Memory (DRAM, SRAM, and EPROM)

- Rotating media (ATA disk drives)

- Solid state disk drives

PC DOS provides PCMCIA support through PhoenixCARD Manager Plus Version 3.01 (PCM+) from Phoenix Technologies, Ltd. PCM+ provides user-friendly, menu-interfaced utilities for the setup, configuration, and maintenance of your system. It stores your configuration in an initialization file, PCM.INI, which you can modify using these utilities.

You install PCMCIA support during installation of PC DOS 7.0. If you did not choose to install PCMCIA at that time, you can use the PC DOS 7 Setup program with the /E switch to install PCMCIA at any time.

Note: *The command-line switches used for PC DOS versions of Phoenix PCMCIA before PC DOS 7.0 are no longer part of the command-line syntax.*

This latest version of PCMCIA provides the following features:

- An Uninstall program that backs up your current system PC DOS and Windows configuration files as PCM files

- A Setup program that enables you to install and customize PCMCIA quickly and easily

- Support for PC DOS multiple configurations

- Support for Microsoft's Flash File System II device driver

- Utilities for managing PC Cards in both PC DOS and Windows environments

- The capability to insert and remove PC Cards without rebooting

- Support for most PCMCIA cards, including Flash memory, SRAM Memory, FAX/Modem, ATA, hard disks, SCSI, LAN and other I/O cards

Before Starting PCMCIA

Before you start the PCMCIA support utility, you should take the following actions:

- Edit your CONFIG.SYS file to remove the RAMBOOST statement (if RAMBOOST already is installed and configured) and the EMM386 statement.

- Uninstall any prior versions of PCMCIA (including Phoenix).

- Find out the number of PCMCIA sockets you have on your computer, including those associated with a docking bay station.

- Find out the full path to the directory where Windows is installed.

- If you are using a memory manager other than EMM386, manually exclude UMB memory for Card Services and ATA support, and then reset your system.

Note: *If you are using multiple configurations, be aware that PCMCIA changes your CONFIG.SYS file and installs itself in the configuration you have designated to start when you turn on your computer. You must boot with the desired environment under which you want PCMCIA to run.*

Setting Up PCMCIA

Before you can use PCMCIA support, you must install the PCMCIA program on your computer. You install PCMCIA only once, unless at some time, PCMCIA is removed from your computer and you need to install it again.

To install PCMCIA, follow these steps:

1. Remove any PC Cards from their sockets in your computer.

2. Type **CD\DOS** and press **Enter** to change to the DOS directory.

3. At the PC DOS command prompt, type **PCMINST** and press **Enter**. A message appears telling you what is going to happen.

4. Press **Y** to answer Yes and continue to process. PCMINST starts, and the Phoenix Card Manager installation screen is displayed. When the program is installed, it automatically starts the PCMSETUP program, which you can use to configure your system.

5. Follow the instructions on the PCMCIA Setup screen to configure your system. When you are finished, press **F3** to exit back to the PC DOS command prompt.

In the future, to change your PCMCIA configuration, type **PCMSETUP** at the PC DOS command prompt to start the PCMCIA Setup program.

Using the MSCDEX Command

CD-ROM

An acronym for compact-disc, read-only memory. CD-ROMs are storage devices that can be read using CD-ROM drives.

PC DOS 7.0 provides support for *CD-ROM* drives. You can use the MSCDEX command to access and control CD-ROM drives attached to your computer.

To use the MSCDEX command to access CD-ROM drives, you first must load the device driver that came with your CD-ROM into the CONFIG.SYS file. For more information, see Chapter 8, "Configuring Your Personal Computer," and the CD-ROM drive documentation.

After you have the device drivers included in your CONFIG.SYS file, you can use the MSCDEX command from the PC DOS command prompt by typing **MSCDEX** and specifying the device driver. You also can add the MSCDEX command to your AUTOEXEC.BAT file so that the command is enabled every time you start your computer. For more information about adding commands to the AUTOEXEC.BAT file, see Chapter 8, "Configuring Your Personal Computer."

To add the MSCDEX command to your AUTOEXEC.BAT file, the command statement must include a /D:*drivename* parameter that matches the /D:*drivename* parameter used in the CONFIG.SYS file for the CD-ROM device driver. Each CD-ROM device driver currently in use must have a unique driver name.

Note: *The device driver for your CD-ROM comes with your CD-ROM, not with PC DOS. To use MSCDEX.EXE in PC DOS to access and use your CD-ROM, you must have the CD-ROM device driver loaded in the CONFIG.SYS file.*

Using REXX

**Programming
language**
Code used to
write computer
programs.

REXX, the REstructured eXtended eXecutor language, is an easy-to-use
yet powerful *programming language* that is an integral part of PC DOS. Its
simplicity makes it a good first language for beginners. For more experienced users, REXX offers powerful functions, extensive mathematical
capabilities, and the capability to issue commands to multiple environments. REXX for PC DOS includes utilities and REXX commands that
have been designed to work specifically with PC DOS. For detailed information about using REXX, consult the *PC DOS 7 REXX User's Guide and
Reference*.

REXX is a programming language that combines the simplicity of a language like BASIC with the capabilities of a more powerful language.
REXX is easy to learn because it uses familiar words and concepts.

REXX uses a few powerful, general-purpose programming functions and
common mathematical abilities, as well as PC DOS commands, within a
simple framework. Existing batch files can be converted to REXX procedures, providing more power and function.

Getting Help for Using REXX

PC DOS provides two ways for you to get more information about the
REXX programming language:

- The on-line book viewer

- DOS Help

To open the DOSREXX on-line book in the PC DOS viewer, at the
PC DOS command prompt, type **VIEW DOSREXX** and press **Enter**.

To view information about a specific REXX command for PC DOS using
PC DOS Help, follow these steps:

1. At the PC DOS command prompt, type **HELP**.

2. Press the **spacebar** once to leave a space between the command
   HELP and the REXX command for which you want to display help.

3. Type the name of the REXX command for which you want to
   display help.

4. Press **Enter**.

For example, to find out more information about the REXX LASTPOS command, type **HELP LASTPOS** at the PC DOS command prompt.

Note: *If the name of the PC DOS command and the REXX command are the same, add rexx preceding the REXX command name, like this:* **HELP REXX REXX***command*.

Using File Update

Synchronized
Exactly the same, according to the most recent changes.

File Update is a new PC DOS program that enables you to compare files on two different computers running PC DOS 7.0. This program is a useful tool because it helps you keep files *synchronized*, no matter where or when you work on them. If you work on a file on one computer at work and on another computer at home, for example, you can use File Update to make sure that both files are up-to-date.

You can use File Update on two separate computers, a computer and a local area network (LAN), or at two different locations on the same computer. You also can use File Update to keep backup files of your work on another drive or partition.

To use File Update, you first must install it on both of the systems you plan to use; then you can transfer files via diskette from one system to the other. One system is called the base system; the other is the remote system. You can transfer updated files back and forth from either system.

Preparing To Use File Update

Before you install File Update on your computer systems, there are a few steps you should take.

First, make sure that the time and date at both locations are the same. File Update uses the PC DOS time and date stamps to keep track of when files are changed. Use the DATE command to check and to change the system date; use the TIME command to check and to change the system time. For more information on using these commands, see Chapter 2, "Making PC DOS Work."

You also must know how files and directories are organized on both your systems. File Update tracks changes that are made to the files and directories you specify.

You must know the following:

- The names and extensions of the files you want tracked. For example, do you want to track all files with a TXT extension, such as REPORT.TXT?

- The directories in which these files are located. For example, are the files stored in C:\COMPUTER\SALES at the base location and D:\SALES at the remote location?

Use the PC DOS TREE command to examine your directory tree to find the answers to these questions. For more information on using the TREE command, see Chapter 2, "Making PC DOS Work."

Installing File Update at the Base Location

To set up File Update, you first install it at the base location. Installing File Update at the base location creates an installation diskette, which you will use to install File Update at the remote location.

Note: *If you are installing File Update on a computer connected to a Local Area Network or to another computer using the PC DOS InterLnk program, use the client system as the base location.*

To install File Update at the base location, follow these steps:

1. At the PC DOS command prompt, type **FILEUP**.

2. Press **Enter**. The File Update utility starts, and the Welcome screen appears.

The File Update Utility has a shell interface similar to other PC DOS tools.

File Update menu bar ———

Click to install ———

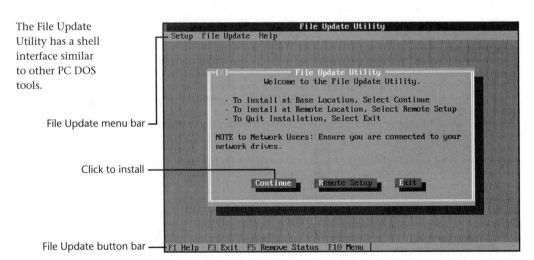

File Update button bar ———

10

If you have problems...	If you receive a Bad command or file name message, you may need to change to the DOS directory before typing the command.

Note: *If File Update appears without a Welcome screen, the program has been installed. To reinstall, select Delete Installation from the Setup menu, and begin again with step 1.*

3. Choose Continue. The Location Names screen is displayed.

You must name the two systems so that File Update can identify them when it compares the files.

Type a name for the base location

Type a name for the remote location

4. In the Name of Base Location text box, type a name for the base location system. For example, if the system is at home, type **HOME**.

5. Press **Tab** to move to the Name of Remote Location text box.

6. In the Name of Remote Location text box, type a name for the remote location system. For example, if the system is at work, type **WORK**.

7. Choose Continue. The Program Path screen is displayed.

You must type the paths to the locations of the File Update program files for both the base location and the remote location so that PC DOS can find the program files on each computer system.

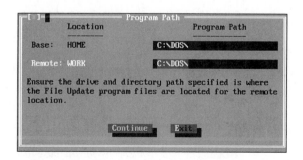

Note: *Use the **Tab** key to move around the text boxes and the command buttons in the File Update utility, or use the mouse to click a text box or a command button.*

8. Make sure that the paths entered in the Program Path text boxes are the correct locations for the File Update program files on each system.

9. Choose Continue. The Add/Delete Directory Pairs screen appears.

You must identify the drive and directory paths where you want File Update to track the file on each system.

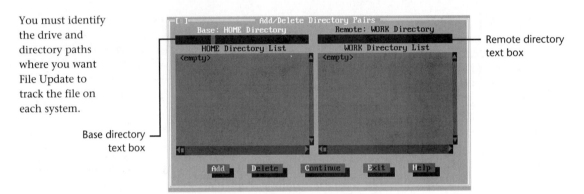

Remote directory text box

Base directory text box

10. In the Base Directory text box, type the drive and directory path, including all subdirectories, where you want File Update to track files on the base computer system.

11. Press **Tab** to move to the Remote Directory text box.

12. In the Remote Directory text box, type the drive and directory path, including all subdirectories, where you want File Update to track the files on the remote computer system.

13. Choose **A**dd. The paths are entered in the appropriate lists.

For example, if you type **C:\COMPUTER\SALES** in the Base Directory text box and **D:\SALES** in the Remote Directory text box, when you transfer the files, File Update tracks the files in the specified directories for updating.

Note: *The path you specify for the base location must exist, but the path specified for the remote location can be created when you transfer updated files.*

> **Tip**
>
> Directory pairs can be the same drive and directory, different drives and directories, or the same drive but different directories. You can add or delete directory pairs at any time.

14. Choose Continue. The Diskette Drive Selection screen is displayed. You now will create a File Update installation diskette to use to install File Update on the remote computer.

15. Choose the diskette drive (drive A or B) where you will insert the blank diskette. Remember that it must fit into a drive on the remote computer, as well.

16. Insert a blank, formatted diskette into the specified drive, and choose Continue.

17. Choose OK when the installation is complete.

18. Label your diskette "File Update Installation," and set it aside.

   Note: *If your remote location is connected through LAN or InterLnk, you do not need to use the File Update Installation diskette again. You need only to remap the drives.*

19. Use the options on the Setup menu to specify the files and directories you want to track.

Note: *The Files Being Excluded choice in the Setup menu contains a default list of file extensions that are not being tracked. Be sure to review this list so that you do not have files missing when you transfer file updates. You can add extensions to the Excluded list so that specific file types are not tracked. You also can delete any file extensions that you want File Update to include in its tracking.*

Installing File Update at the Remote Location

To install File Update on a remote computer that is not connected to a LAN or to another computer, follow these steps:

Note: *You have to follow this procedure only the first time you transfer files.*

1. At the PC DOS command prompt on the remote PC, type **FILEUP** to start the File Update utility.

2. Press **Enter**. The Welcome screen appears.

3. Choose Remote Setup.

4. Insert the File Update Installation diskette you created on your base system into drive A or B.

5. Specify the drive where you inserted the diskette, and choose **C**ontinue. PC DOS installs File Update on the remote computer.

6. Choose OK when the installation is complete.

7. Use the options on the Setup menu to specify the files and directories you want File Update to track.

Transferring Updated Files

After you install File Update, you can work with the files on either computer and then copy them to diskettes to transfer to the other computer. The procedure is the same on both the remote and the base systems.

To transfer files from the computer to the diskette, follow these steps:

1. Start the File Update utility.

2. Choose **F**ile Update, Update **T**o Diskette.

3. Choose Update Files.

4. Follow the instructions on your screen. Insert a blank formatted diskette into the specified drive. File Update copies to the diskette all the files it has been tracking.

Note: *You may need more than one diskette. Label the diskettes carefully— you must insert them in the correct order when you update the files on the other computer.*

To transfer files from the diskette to the computer at the other location, follow these steps:

1. Start the File Update utility.

2. Choose **F**ile Update, Update **F**rom Diskette.

3. Choose Update Files.

4. Follow the instructions on your screen. Insert the last diskette of the set that contains the updated files you transferred. Continue inserting the diskettes until the transfer is complete.

10

Using InterLnk

With the InterLnk utility program and a cable, you can connect one computer to another computer so that you can transfer files between computers or use one computer to run programs located on another computer.

InterLnk is designed specifically to enable you to exchange files between any two types of computers that can be connected by cables. You can connect a laptop computer to a desktop computer or a desktop computer, for example, to another desktop computer.

To use InterLnk, you need the following:

- Two computers running PC DOS Version 5.02 or higher. Running this version of PC DOS ensures that both the INTERLNK.EXE and INTERSVR.EXE files are available.

Caution
Plugging a parallel cable into a serial connector or vice versa will damage your computer system.

- An available serial or parallel port on each computer. Your cable connection must be serial-to-serial or parallel-to-parallel; if you have an available serial port, the second computer also must have an available serial port.

- A type of connecting serial or parallel cable.

- 16K of free memory on the client computer and 130K of free memory on the server computer.

- The INTERLNK.EXE device driver statement `device=c:\dos\interlnk.exe` in your CONFIG.SYS file on the designated client computer.

Understanding InterInk

Client

When computers are connected by cables or on a LAN, the computer you use to enter commands and perform tasks.

Server

When computers are connected by cables or on a LAN, the computer dedicated to providing resources to client computers.

Using the InterLnk program, you create what is called a *client/server* relationship between two computers.

The computer you use to enter commands is called the client. The client is usually your own computer or the computer you use most frequently.

The computer connected to the client is called the server because it is dedicated to serving the client. The server computer runs the file-transfer program and the INTERSVR.EXE program. The client runs the INTERLNK.EXE program.

After a connection is made to the server computer, the client computer assumes that the server computer's drives and printers are its own. You use your own computer—the client computer—as you normally use it, or you use the client computer to access data on the server computer. The display of the server computer displays the status of the connection. You use the server computer keyboard only to break the connection between the two computers.

For more information about INTERLNK or INTERLNK.EXE, see your on-line PC DOS 7.0 Command Reference. Or type **HELP INTERLNK** at the PC DOS command prompt. For a list of the options available with INTERSVR, type **HELP INTERSVR** at the PC DOS command prompt.

Running the InterInk Program

After you have connected your computers by attaching the appropriate cables to the appropriate ports, you can run the InterLnk program.

To start InterInk, follow these steps:

1. On the server computer, to make a serial connection, type **INTERSVR**.

   To make a parallel connection, type **INTERSVR /LPT1**.

   You see a screen displaying the server drives.

   Note: *If you are running Windows, you see a task-swapping message; if you are running PC DOS, you do not see this message. Press **Enter** to continue, or press **F3** to quit.*

2. At the PC DOS command prompt of the client computer, type
INTERLNK and press **Enter**. This command verifies that
the InterLnk program is loaded and displays the status of the
connections.

You now can access the drives of the server computer as though
they were located on your client computer. If you need different
drives from the ones currently accessed, redirect the drives.

3. When you are finished, press **Alt+F4** on the server to break the
connection. The server returns to the PC DOS command prompt,
and the client no longer has access to the server's drives.

10

Chapter 11

Using Stacker Compression

It seems that no matter how much disk space you have when you first get a computer, you soon need more. Windows and Windows applications generally are large programs that require large amounts of disk space to run on a computer.

When you run out of disk space, you have a few options:

- You can delete some of your data.

- You can buy another disk.

- You can compress your data so that more fits into the same amount of space.

Data compression

The process of reducing the number of bytes required to represent data so that the data consumes less disk space.

Caution

Compression is a feature that only knowledgeable users should attempt. This chapter is just an overview of data compression.

Data compression is accomplished by using a data-compression software utility. PC DOS comes with a data-compression utility, Stacker, that can be used from Windows or DOS.

Stacker uses a patented compression technique that can more than double the capacity of your disks. In addition, Stacker takes advantage of compression features built into PC DOS 7.0. It automatically converts disks that have been compressed with DoubleSpace/DriveSpace, SuperStor/DS, or versions of Stacker other than Stacker for OS/2 and DOS.

In this chapter, you learn how to use Stacker to compress your data and increase your disk drive capacity.

Understanding Stacker

Byte

A measurement of information stored on a disk. One byte is equal to approximately one character.

The amount of data that can fit on a storage disk is measured in *bytes*— one byte equals approximately one character. Every disk holds a specific number of bytes. When the disk is full, you cannot store even a single additional byte on it. (See Chapter 1, "Understanding System Basics," for more information about disks and disk capacities.)

Stacker gives you more disk space by compressing files so that they take up less space. Stacker's patented data-compression technique— Stacker LZS—eliminates repetitive information from your files. And, Stacker SmartPack tightly packs your files into spaces on your disk that DOS cannot access without Stacker's help.

Unlike other compression products, Stacker monitors your compression. If your data compression ratio is better than 2.5:1, Stacker adjusts your actual compression ratio to reflect the improvement, giving you the most space possible.

After you set up Stacker and more than double your disk space, you still use your computer just as you did before. The only difference is that you have a great deal more space on your disk.

The files required for you to start Stacker are loaded onto your system during the installation and setup of PC DOS.

> **Tip**
>
> If you did not select Stacker Compression at the initial installation of PC DOS 7.0, you still can install this optional tool by rerunning PC DOS Setup using the /E switch. Insert the Setup diskette from the PC DOS installation diskettes into drive A or B. Then, at the DOS command prompt, type **A:SETUP /E** or **B:SETUP /E**. Follow the instructions displayed on-screen to install Stacker Compression. For more information about installing the PC DOS tools, consult your PC DOS 7.0 User's Guide.

Some situations in which you might want to use the Stacker data-compression program follow:

■ You do not have enough space on your desktop computer's hard disk to install new application programs or utilities.

- When you try to store a file, you receive one of these messages: `Not Enough Disk Space` or `Disk Full`.

- Your laptop or notebook does not have enough storage space to load and run all the programs you require.

- You do not want to invest in upgrading your equipment only because your hard disk is not large enough.

- You want to store more data on one diskette.

Stacker frees up more of your disk space and makes it easy to monitor your drives from the Stacker DOS toolbox or the new Stacker Windows toolbox.

Stacker also offers the following features:

- Enables you to take data on compressed disks anywhere, even if the computer does not have Stacker installed, using Stacker Anywhere.

- Instantly converts other compressed drives. The resulting Stacker drives give you more space than either DoubleSpace/DriveSpace or Superstor/DS.

- Uses as little memory as possible.

- Stacker DOS Toolbox tools show you extra bytes, free space, and fragmentation. All Stacker's tools are on an easy-to-use menu in the toolbox.

- Guards your data. Every time you start up your system, Stacker runs AutoProtect to make sure that your data is in good condition. Stacker AutoSave, available only through the Windows toolbox, backs up important file-access information.

- Shows you how much data needs to be backed up. The new Backup Status gauge, available only through the Windows toolbox, keeps track for you.

- Flashes or plays sounds to remind you of disk-maintenance tasks. You can set up the Stacker Windows toolbox to tell you when the disk is getting full, when it is time to back up files, or when you should optimize your disk.

Note: *You can access Stacker's comprehensive on-line help with one press of a key or a click of your mouse. During Stacker Setup, press **F1** or click on* Help. *Using the Stacker DOS toolbox, press **F1**. Using the Stacker Windows toolbox, choose **T**oolbox Help from the **H**elp menu or press **F1** to get context-sensitive help on any dialog box or screen. For help on general topics, double-click on the Stacker Help icon in the Stacker Windows Program group.*

Setting Up Stacker

Setting up Stacker is easy. First, you run the SSETUP Stacker Setup program to prepare your drives for data compression. While running SSETUP for the initial installation of Stacker, the Stacker directory and files are moved from C:\DOS\STACKER to C:\STACKER, and your hard drive C is compressed.

After that, just use Stacker's SETUP command or the Stacker Toolbox tools to compress any additional drives.

Early on in the Stacker Setup procedure, Stacker asks whether you want to use Express Setup or Custom Setup. Think about the following guidelines to make your selection.

Choose Express Setup to

- Set up Stacker quickly and easily.

- Set up Stacker on all hard disks or partitions larger than 5M.

- Let Stacker make the decisions for your system.

Choose Custom Setup to

- Set up Stacker on one disk or partition at a time.

- Compress only the free space left on the disk. Stacker asks you how much free space you want to reserve as uncompressed space.

- Control options such as whether to use Expanded Memory Specification (EMS), the cluster size of your Stacker drives, or how much space to leave uncompressed.

Note: *Unless you are very knowledgeable about your computer system, you should use Express Setup.*

Note: *Before you run the Stacker Setup program, you should back up your data. Stacker is completely safe and does not harm your data. Still, before making any system change, it is always a good idea to back up your data. If you have a backup routine, just follow it, but do a complete backup. If you use a tape backup, do a file-by-file backup (not an image backup). For information on backing up, see Chapter 10, "Using PC DOS 7.0 Tools."*

Starting the Stacker Setup Program the First Time

You can start the Stacker Setup program from DOS or Windows. If you start from Windows, however, after the first few screens, Stacker leaves Windows to complete the installation procedure and compress your disks.

Note: *If you plan to use Stacker with Windows, you should install Windows before installing Stacker so that your Stacker Windows group is set up automatically for you. If you install Stacker first and then install Windows, use the Stacker SGROUP command to create the Stacker Windows group. Type **HELP SGROUP** at the PC DOS command prompt to see complete information.*

Starting Stacker from DOS

To start Stacker from DOS, follow these steps:

1. At the PC DOS command prompt, type **SSETUP** and press **Enter**.

    The welcome screen appears.

Stacker Setup uses a GUI interface like other DOS tools. The Stacker Welcome screen advises you to back up your data before continuing.

Click to continue ──

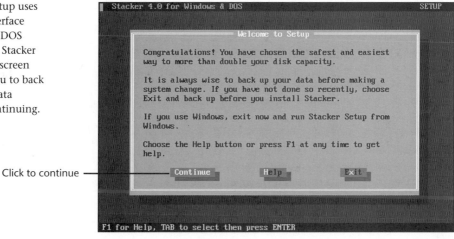

2. Click **C**ontinue.

Stacker displays the Express or Custom Setup? screen.

Unless you are very confident about configuring your computer system, you should use Express Setup to set up Stacker.

```
Stacker 4.0 for Windows & DOS                                    SETUP
 ═══════════════ Express or Custom Setup? ═══════════════
  Stacker offers two setup methods.

  Express Setup

      Express compresses data on ALL your hard
      disks and makes the best choices for your
      system.

  Custom Setup

      Custom compresses the disk you select and
      lets you make all the choices for your
      configuration.

         Express     Custom     Help     Exit

 F1 for Help, TAB to select then press ENTER
```

Click to start Express Setup

Click to exit back to the PC DOS command prompt

3. Click **E**xpress.

The Express Setup screen appears.

At this point, the rest of the procedure is the same, whether you started Stacker from DOS or from Windows. Continue reading with the section "Completing Stacker Setup."

Note: *If your computer has an LCD, grayscale, or monochrome monitor, type* **SSETUP /M** *so that you can read the screens easier.*

Starting Stacker from Windows

To start Stacker from the Windows Program Manager, follow these steps:

1. Start Windows.

2. In the Program Manager, open the **F**ile menu and choose **R**un.

3. In the Command Line field, type **SSETUP**.

4. Click OK or press **Enter**.

The welcome screen appears.

In Windows, the
Stacker screens
conform to
Windows stan-
dards, but they
offer the same
choices as
Stacker for DOS.

Click to continue ⎯⎯⎯⎯⎯⎯

Click to exit back to
the Program Manager

5. Click OK.

Stacker displays the Express or Custom Setup? screen. The Express
Setup option already is selected.

You can choose
Express Setup or
Custom Setup
when starting
Stacker from
Windows.

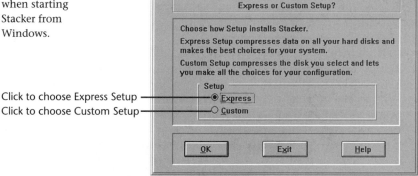

Click to choose Express Setup ⎯⎯⎯⎯
Click to choose Custom Setup ⎯⎯⎯⎯

6. Click OK to start Express Setup.

The Express Setup screen appears.

7. Click OK.

The Leave Windows screen appears.

8. Click OK.

Stacker leaves Windows to complete the installation procedure and disk compression from the PC DOS command prompt. The rest of the procedure is the same as if you had started Stacker from the PC DOS command prompt.

Completing Stacker Setup

Whether you start Stacker from DOS or from Windows, once the Express Setup screen is displayed, the rest of the setup procedure is the same.

The first time you use Stacker Setup, the Stacker files are copied into the \STACKER directory.

Confirm the Stacker directory

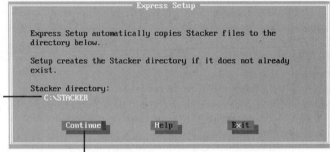

Click to continue setting up Stacker on your hard drive

To continue setting up Stacker and compressing your hard disk C, follow these steps:

1. In the Express Setup screen, click Continue.

Stacker copies the Stacker files to the C:\STACKER directory and displays the Start Compressing screen.

PC DOS must restart your computer in order to complete the installation of Stacker on your hard disk.

Click to continue setting up Stacker

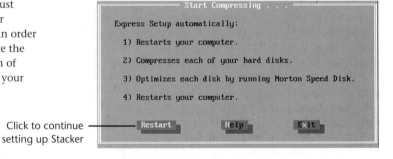

2. Click **R**estart.

Stacker restarts your computer to collect disk information it needs to compress your disks. It also disables any programs loaded in memory by AUTOEXEC.BAT that might interfere with the disk compression. It then creates a Stacker drive on your hard drive C. When the compression is complete, Stacker displays the Express Setup Results screen, which shows you the results of the compression.

3. Press **Enter**.

Stacker restarts your computer again and displays the PC DOS command prompt.

You can continue using DOS, Windows, and your PC the same way you did before using Stacker, but now you have more room on your hard disk to store files.

Compressing Additional Disks

After you use SSETUP to set up Stacker the first time, you can use the Stacker Setup program to compress additional drives.

To compress additional drives, follow these steps:

1. At the PC DOS command prompt, type **CD\STACKER** and press **Enter** to change to the Stacker subdirectory.

2. Type **SETUP** to start the Stacker compression program.

3. Follow the instructions displayed on your screen to compress additional drives.

You also can compress additional drives using the Stacker DOS or Windows toolbox. See "Using Stacker Tools," later in this chapter, for more information.

Upgrading Existing Stacker Drives

When you run Stacker Setup, it detects any earlier versions of Stacker on your system and offers you two options: Full Update or Quick Update. Full Update is a thorough upgrade for your entire system. It updates earlier Stacker files, defragments the drive, and recompresses the data using

Stacker's compression technology. It can take as long as a few hours, but it gives you the best compression. Quick Update updates earlier files but does not defragment or recompress any files on the drive.

Converting DoubleSpace or DriveSpace Drives

Stacker Setup automatically converts DBLSPACE or DRVSPACE drives to Stacker drives, if the drives were compressed by the following:

- PC DOS's SuperStor/DS (Versions 6.1 and 6.3)

- Microsoft's DoubleSpace (Versions 6.0 and 6.2)

- Microsoft's DriveSpace (Version 6.2.2)

Mount
To make available for use—a term applied to disks and disk drives.

Make sure that the drives are *mounted* before running Stacker Setup. Refer to your original compression product's documentation for mounting details.

Caution

Stacker and another compression program cannot both work on the same system. After you install Stacker, you will not have access to the data on un-mounted drives compressed by other products. You first must mount the drives, temporarily or permanently, and then run DCONVERT or HCONVERT (for previous versions of Stacker). For information about these commands, see "Stacker Command Summary," later in this chapter.

Using Stacker Tools

Stacker comes with all the tools you need to monitor the status of your drives and to make changes to your Stacker drives. You can access the Stacker Toolbox from DOS to perform Stacker tasks when you are not using Windows, and you can access the Stacker Toolbox from Windows when you are using Windows, to get drive information and perform Stacker tasks.

You can use the commands in the Stacker Toolbox to check the integrity of your compressed drives and to display a compression report. The Toolbox also contains tools that make it simple for you to use the most common Stacker features and commands, such as compressing and uncompressing drives. For more information about all the Stacker commands, see "Stacker Command Summary," later in this chapter.

Using the Stacker Toolbox from DOS

To open the Stacker DOS Toolbox, follow these steps:

1. At the PC DOS command prompt, type **CD\STACKER** and press **Enter** to change to the Stacker directory.

2. Type **STAC** and press **Enter**.

The Stacker toolbox opens.

The Stacker toolbox gives you quick access to the most common Stacker commands and features.

Toolbox commands —

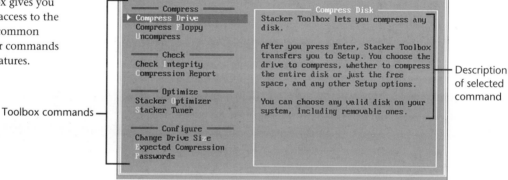

Description of selected command

On the left side of the Stacker Toolbox screen, Stacker lists the available command options. On the right side of the Toolbox screen, Stacker describes the currently highlighted option.

To choose an option in the DOS toolbox, use the up- and down-arrow keys to highlight the option name; then press **Enter**.

To display help, press **F1**.

To exit the toolbox and return to the PC DOS command prompt, press **F10**. Stacker asks you to confirm that you want to exit. Press **Enter** to choose Yes.

Using the Stacker Toolbox from Windows

To open the Stacker Windows toolbox, follow these steps:

1. Start Windows. If you have just run Stacker Setup for the first time, Windows prompts you to set up the Stacker program group. Click OK to go ahead and set up the program group.

2. In the Program Manager, double-click the Stacker program icon to open the Stacker program group window if it is not already open.

Windows creates the Stacker program group after you run Stacker Setup the first time.

Double-click to open the Stacker toolbox

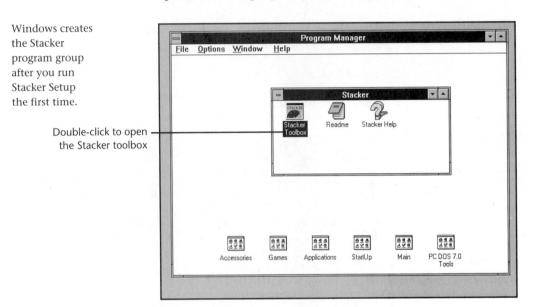

3. Double-click the Stacker Toolbox icon.

The Stacker toolbox opens.

Choose a disk drive

Disk Space gauge

Fragmentation level

Backup status

The Stacker Windows toolbox displays information about the current Stacker drive.

Stacker tool buttons

Compression Ratio gauge

Status bar

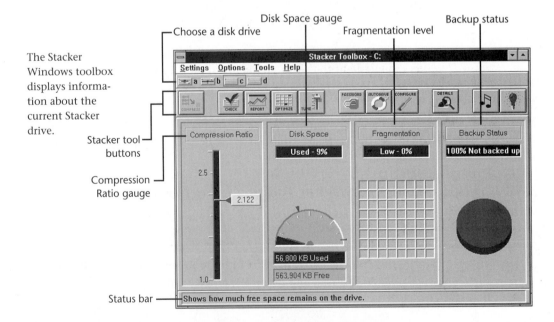

The compression ratio, disk space usage, fragmentation, and current backup status of the selected disk are shown in the Toolbox window. To see the status of a different drive, click the drive icon at the top of screen.

All the Stacker commands are represented by icons. To find out what each icon does, point at it with your mouse; a description appears in the status bar at the bottom of the Toolbox window. To use a command, click the appropriate icon. For more information on each command, see "Stacker Command Summary," later in this chapter.

Note: *You can manipulate the Toolbox window the same way you manipulate other program windows. You can move it, resize it, and minimize or maximize it. To close the window, double-click the Control menu button at the top left of the window title bar. For more information on using windows, see Chapter 3, "Working with the Windows Desktop" and Chapter 4, "Making Windows Work."*

Monitoring Your Stacker Drives

The same processes in your computer system that cause DOS-related problems also may cause Stacker drive problems. It is a good idea to check your drive regularly to find and fix problems that may occur.

By using the tools in the Stacker toolbox, you can monitor your drives from DOS or Windows. You can check the integrity of your Stacker disks, and you can display a compression report describing the status of your Stacker disks. In DOS, you can check the data integrity and the disk integrity and, if you find problems, you can fix them. In Windows, you can check the data integrity. You must return to DOS to fix problems.

Checking Drive Integrity from DOS

From DOS, you can check the integrity of the data on your Stacker drives and the integrity of the drive itself. During the check, Stacker prompts you to fix problems that it finds.

To check the integrity of your Stacker drives from DOS, follow these steps:

1. At the PC DOS command prompt, type **CD\STACKER** and press **Enter** to change to the Stacker subdirectory.

2. Type **STAC** and press **Enter** to open the Stacker toolbox.

3. Press the **down arrow** to highlight Check Integrity.

   This option enables you to check a Stacker drive for problems.

4. Press **Enter**.

   Stacker checks the integrity of the data on the disk, and then asks whether you want to perform a Disk Surface test to check the integrity of the disk itself.

5. Take one of the following actions:

   Press **Y** and then **Enter** to check the disk. A Surface test can take some time, so you should press Y only if you will not need to use your computer for a while.

   Press **N** and then **Enter** to skip the Surface test.

6. If Stacker finds a problem, it prompts you to fix it. It may suggest that you use the CHECK command with the /F switch from the PC DOS command prompt, or it may suggest that you use the CHKDSK command with the /F switch from the PC DOS command prompt. Follow the recommendation to fix the problem.

When you are done checking disk integrity, Stacker displays the DOS toolbox again.

Checking Data Integrity from Windows

To check the integrity of the data on your Stacker disk from Windows, follow these steps:

1. Start Windows.

2. Open the Stacker program group window.

3. Open the Stacker toolbox.

4. Click the icon for the drive you want to check.

5. Click the Check tool icon.

   Stacker checks your disk, and then displays the drive compression ratio.

Stacker returns to
DOS to check the
integrity of the
data on your disk.
You must exit back
to Windows.

Drive compression ratio ─┐

Amount of free ─┐
space on drive

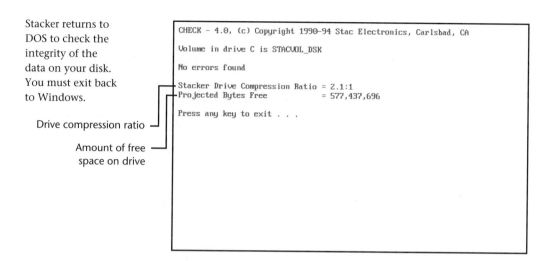

```
CHECK - 4.0, (c) Copyright 1990-94 Stac Electronics, Carlsbad, CA

Volume in drive C is STACVOL_DSK

No errors found

Stacker Drive Compression Ratio = 2.1:1
Projected Bytes Free            = 577,437,696

Press any key to exit . . .
```

11

6. Press any key to return to the Stacker Windows toolbox.

Displaying a Compression Report from DOS

You can use the Stacker DOS toolbox to display a detailed compression
report about your Stacker disk. You can view the compression status of
files on your Stacker disk, or you can change the view to show summary
information about the disk.

To display a compression report from DOS, follow these steps:

1. At the PC DOS command prompt, type **CD\STACKER** and press
Enter to change to the Stacker subdirectory.

2. Type **STAC** and press **Enter** to open the Stacker Toolbox.

3. Press the **down arrow** to highlight Compression Report and
then press **Enter**.

Stacker displays a report.

Click to show a summary report

Click to show a report for a different drive

The Compression report provides statistics about the amount of disk space used by different types of files, and about the compression ratio levels.

Click to change the Sort category

Click to change the Sort order

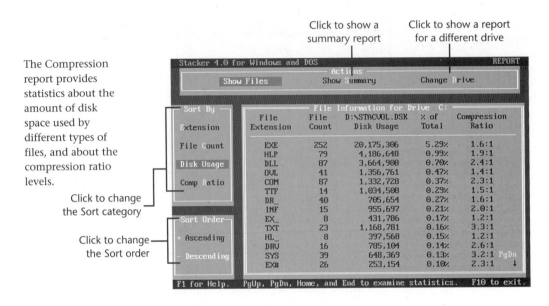

Because files of a specific type usually are compressed in a similar manner, and because file types can be identified by file extension, Stacker displays information about files according to file extension. It lists the number of files with each extension, the amount of disk space used by those files, and the compression ratio for those files.

By default, the files are sorted in ascending order by disk usage. You can change the sort order by using the up- and down-arrow keys to choose a different category and sort order.

4. Click Show **S**ummary to display the Summary Information report.

The Summary report provides easy-to-read statistics about your Stacker drives.

Click to view the compression report

Compression ratio statistics

Disk space statistics

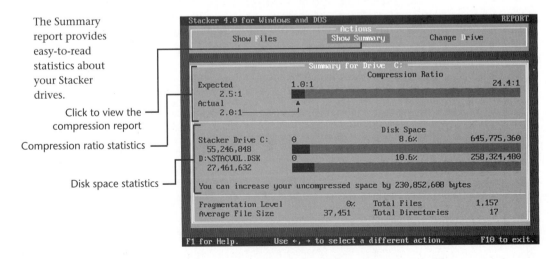

5. Press **F10**, and then press **Enter** to exit back to the Stacker DOS toolbox.

Displaying Compression Information from Windows

In the Stacker Windows toolbox, a great deal of information about your Stacker drive is displayed in the Toolbox window: You can see the compression ratio, the amount of used disk space, the fragmentation status, and the backup status. If you want to display more comprehensive information about the disk, you can use the Report tool or the Details tool.

To see summary information about the way disk space is used, follow these steps:

1. Start Windows.

2. Open the Stacker program group window.

3. Open the Stacker toolbox.

4. Click the icon for the drive on which you want to report.

5. Click the Details icon.

   Stacker displays a Disk Space Details box, which shows a graphic representation of your disk.

6. Click OK to return to the Stacker Windows toolbox.

The Details tool shows a graphic representation of your disk and the way data is stored on your disk.

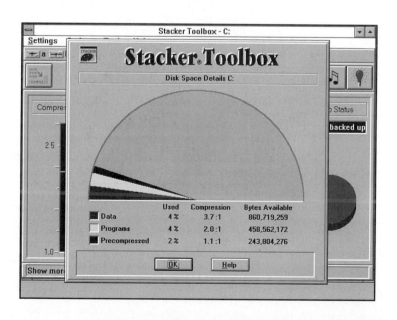

To display a Compression report for your Stacker disks from Windows, follow these steps:

1. Start Windows.

2. Open the Stacker program group window.

3. Open the Stacker toolbox.

4. Click the icon for the drive on which you want to report.

5. Click the Report icon.

Stacker displays a report detailing information about the files on the drive.

In Windows, compression data is arranged by file type. By default, it is sorted by number of bytes.

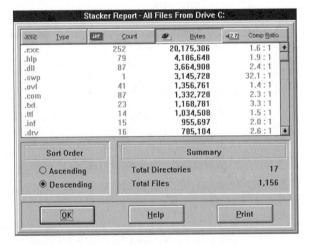

6. Click OK to return to the Stacker Windows toolbox.

Table 11.1 describes the commands included in the Stacker toolboxes.

Table 11.1 Commands in the Stacker Toolboxes	
Command	**Function**
Change Drive Size	Increases the size of the Stacker drive or makes more compressed space available.
Check Integrity	Checks the integrity of data on a Stacker drive and of the drive itself.

Command	Function
Compress Drive	Runs Stacker Setup to compress additional hard disks or diskettes.
Compress Floppy	Compresses the available free space on a diskette.
Compression Report	Displays statistics about compression and disk usage.
Expected Compression	Changes the expected compression ratio for a Stacker drive.
Passwords	Assigns a password to restrict access to your Stacker drive, or removes an existing password.
Stacker Optimizer	Defragments or recompresses data on a Stacker drive.
Stacker Tuner	Adjusts the balance between how tightly and how quickly Stacker compresses data.
Uncompress	Uncompresses a Stacker drive and reverses the Stacker Setup process.

Stacker Command Summary

You can use many commands with Stacker to change the way Stacker works. The most common commands are included in the DOS and Windows toolboxes so that you can access them quickly and easily.

You can use other commands from the PC DOS command line. Table 11.2 provides an overview of the Stacker commands that you can use from the PC DOS command line.

For more information about Stacker commands, use DOS Help. Just type **HELP**, followed by the command name at the PC DOS command line. DOS then displays detailed information about the command's syntax and usage. To get help on using the CHECK command, for example, type **HELP CHECK** and press **Enter**.

Note: *To use the Stacker commands, you must change to the directory that contains your Stacker files—usually the \STACKER directory. If you plan to use these commands often, you may want to add the \STACKER directory to the PATH statement in your CONFIG.SYS file. For more information, see Chapter 8, "Configuring Your Personal Computer."*

Table 11.2 Stacker Commands

Command	Function
CHECK	Checks a Stacker compressed drive, produces a status report, and fixes detected problems.
CONFIG	Creates Stacker lines in the system configuration files.
CREATE	Creates an empty Stacker drive using available disk space.
DBLSPACE	Calls the DBLSPACE menu-driven interface.
DCONVERT	Converts a DoubleSpace or SuperStor/DS compressed drive into a Stacker drive.
DPMS	Loads the Stacker driver into extended memory.
HCONVERT	Updates an earlier version of a Stacker drive that was not mounted when you first ran Stacker Setup, or updates a removable Stacker drive.
PASSWD	Sets read/write or read-only passwords for Stacker drives.
REMOVDRV	Deletes the Stacker STACVOL file and all the data it contains from the specified Stacker drive.
REPORT	Displays statistics for Stacker drives.
RESIZE	Changes the size of the Stacker drive. If you increase the size of the Stacker drive, the uncompressed drive becomes smaller; if you add space to the uncompressed drive, the amount of space available in the STACVOL.*xxx* file for compressed files becomes smaller.
SCREATE	Compresses RAM drives. This command can be used only in the CONFIG.SYS file.
SDEFRAG	Runs the Stacker Optimizer to defragment or recompress a Stacker drive.
SDIR	Displays the compression ratio for a list of files and directories.
SETUP	Prepares drives and compresses disks.
SGROUP	Creates a Windows program group.
SSETUP	Activates the Stacker installation program to prepare disks for compression.
STAC	Opens the Stacker DOS toolbox.
STACHIGH	Loads Stacker into high memory. A statement must be added to the CONFIG.SYS file before this can take effect.
STACKER	Mounts or unmounts Stacker drives, or displays the Stacker drive map, which displays the names and locations of Stacker drives.
STACWIN	Opens the Stacker utility program in Windows.
SYSINFO	Gathers and displays information about your computer system.

Command	Function
TUNER	Displays the Stacker Tuner screen, from which you can adjust the balance of compression speed and compression ratio for Stacker drives.
UNCOMP	Uncompresses all the data stored in a Stacker drive and stores it on the original uncompressed disk.

11

Troubleshooting Stacker

A few general procedures can solve virtually any problem you might have with a Stacker drive. In this section, you learn about the following:

- General tips and procedures for running the DOS CHKDSK utility, removing attributes from STACVOL files, and running other disk-repair utilities

- Troubleshooting during Stacker Setup

- Troubleshooting during startup

- Troubleshooting other Stacker problems

Problems are described in a question-and-answer format to help you understand the problems you might be having, as well as the steps you need to take to fix the problems.

General Tips and Procedures

How can I secure my compressed data and fix problems?

Stacker's AutoProtect feature runs every time you start your computer. It scans all Stacker drives on the system and quickly checks the status of each. AutoProtect can fix some problems immediately, so that you never even know they existed. Other problems may be more serious. If AutoProtect cannot repair a problem on a Stacker drive, Stacker write-protects the disk so that your data will not be damaged and then reports to you. Stacker may suggest that you run CHECK /F to correct the problem.

What can I do if my Stacker drive is corrupted?

Running the Stacker CHECK program is always a good first step. If the Stacker drive is corrupted, the CHECK.COM file may be damaged. You can run CHECK from your Stacker startup diskette (if you created one) or from the uncompressed drive. CHECK is the only way to remove write protection from a Stacker drive.

What should I do first to solve system problems?

You can solve some system problems by running the DOS CHKDSK program. Running CHKDSK also runs CHECK on a Stacker compressed drive. You can use CHKDSK to make repairs. Back up damaged files, if you can, before running CHKDSK. For information on how to use CHKDSK, see Chapter 2, "Making PC DOS Work." If CHKDSK reports `Errors with lost allocation units` use CHKDSK with the /F switch to fix all errors. If CHKDSK finds other errors, use a complete disk-repair utility to fix them.

On your Stacker drives, Stacker CHECK runs after DOS CHKDSK finishes. If it offers to do a Disk Surface test, press **Y** for Yes and press **Enter**.

What do I have to do before using a disk-repair utility program?

A multipurpose disk-repair utility can locate hard disk errors, repair many errors, and block out areas of the disk that are bad. If Stacker has write-protected the drive, run CHECK /F to remove the write protection. You will have to run the disk-repair utility on the uncompressed drive that holds the Stacker drive. To do this, change the attributes of the STACVOL file that holds your Stacker drive.

What if I have to remove attributes from a Stacker drive file?

A Stacker drive is contained in a STACVOL file. You may have to remove hidden, system, and read-only attributes from it to correct errors or to run a surface scan. To remove attributes from a STACVOL file, follow these steps:

1. At the PC DOS command prompt, identify the full STACVOL file name from a displayed message, or by typing **STACKER**.

2. Change to the host drive and type the following at the PC DOS command prompt:

   attrib -r -s -h *drive:*stacvol.*xxx*

where *drive:* is the drive and *xxx* is the extension of the STACVOL file.

How can I run a disk-repair utility?

To run a disk-repair utility, follow these steps:

1. Change to the uncompressed drive that contains the STACVOL file.

2. Make the STACVOL file accessible by removing its attributes (see the preceding question and answer).

3. Unmount the Stacker drive by typing the following:

   STACKER *-drive:*

   where *drive:* is the mounted drive letter.

4. Start your disk-repair utility and follow its instructions.

5. Restart your computer.

After your computer restarts, Stacker reapplies the attributes and mounts the Stacker drive.

How can I unmount my Stacker drive to use a disk-repair utility?

Some disk-repair utilities cannot work while a Stacker drive is mounted. If you have to unmount a Stacker drive, type the following at the PC DOS command prompt:

   STACKER *-drive:*

where *-drive:* is the Stacker drive to be unmounted.

When you have finished using the Repair utility, restart your computer to automatically remount the drive.

Troubleshooting During Stacker Setup

Whenever you get an error message during Stacker Setup, you can press **F1** to display context-sensitive help. The Help screen guides you through the steps you should take to work through the problem. During Stacker Setup, if it is safe to stop the procedure, an Exit command button is displayed. However, Stacker provides safeguards in case Stacker Setup is interrupted at some other point.

What can I do if Stacker Setup is interrupted?

Stacker AutoRecover keeps your data safe if Stacker Setup is interrupted for some reason. AutoRecover may complete the compression process or it may remove Stacker compression from the disk, depending on the stage in progress when Stacker Setup was interrupted.

To let AutoRecover take over, follow these steps:

1. Remove any disk from drive A and restart your computer.

2. When Stacker Setup messages appear, follow the instructions. If it offers to decompress data, let it.

3. When the PC DOS command prompt returns, run a disk-repair utility or CHKDSK, and then restart your computer.

4. Run Stacker Setup again, if necessary.

What if Stacker Setup is interrupted or the power goes out while Stacker is creating a Stacker drive?

If Stacker was finished compressing your data when the power went out, or Setup was interrupted for any other reason, restart your system. Setup continues verifying your Stacker drive and completes Setup for that drive. If Stacker was not finished compressing your data, when you restart your system Stacker prompts you to choose between decompressing or leaving the drive as is. If you choose to decompress, your system is restored to its original state. Do not choose to leave the drive as is unless you are comfortable making changes manually.

Troubleshooting During System Startup

When your computer runs, the Stacker driver controls any Stacker drives. If your computer does not start normally, you may not be able to access the data on Stacker drives. The information in this section should help you resolve any problems you encounter during system startup.

Creating a Stacker Startup Diskette

Many problems with compressed data result from errors in the DOS file system or defects in the hard-disk media. When Stacker detects either type of problem, it write-protects your disk to protect your data and suggests how to fix the problem.

One of the best precautions you can take to protect your data from a system failure is to have a Stacker Startup diskette—a bootable diskette that is Stacker-aware. If your system has compressed data files, all the files your system needs for rebooting are available on this diskette.

You can create your own Stacker-aware startup diskette in the event of a system emergency. Keep this startup diskette in case your system ever has a problem. You will be able to start your system from this disk; it will know about Stacker and provide access to your data.

When all else fails, you always can start your system using the PC DOS startup diskette. This method gets you to the PC DOS command prompt. You cannot troubleshoot your machine under Windows.

To create a Stacker startup diskette, follow these steps:

1. Insert a blank unformatted diskette into drive A.

   The capacity of the diskette must be larger than 720K to hold the files you need to copy.

2. Type **FORMAT A: /S /U** and press **Enter** to create a formatted diskette containing the operating system files.

3. Type **A:** and press **Enter** to make drive A the working drive.

4. Use the DOSKey program or type the following commands to copy some additional essential DOS files to the diskette:

   > **COPY C:\DOS\E.EXE**
   >
   > **COPY C:\DOS\ATTRIB.EXE**
   >
   > **COPY C:\DOS\CHKDSK.COM**
   >
   > **COPY C:\DOS\DEFRAG.EXE**
   >
   > **COPY C:\DOS\FORMAT.COM**

   Now, use the ATTRIB command to unhide some of the files you need so that you can copy them to your diskette.

   Note: *Make sure that you are at the A:\> prompt before you begin typing.*

5. Type **C:** to change to the host drive and type the following at the PC DOS command prompt:

   ATTRIB -r -s -h *drive:filename.xxx*

   where *drive:* is the drive where your compression files are located and *filename.xxx* is the name and extension of the file or STACVOL to be copied.

   If you need to see your system's drive mapping, type **STACKER** at the PC DOS command prompt.

6. Type **A:** to make drive A the working drive. Then use the DOSKey program or type the following commands to copy some essential compression files to your diskette. (This example assumes that your files are on drive C and that your STACKER.INI file is on drive G.)

   Note: *Make sure that you are at the A:\> prompt before you begin typing.*

   COPY C:\DOS\STACKER\CHECK.EXE

   COPY C:\DOS\STACKER\CONFIG.EXE

   COPY C:\DOS\STACKER\STACKER.COM

   COPY C:\DOS\STACKER\STACKER2.BIN

   COPY C:\DOS\STACKER\STACVOL.XXX

   COPY C:\DOS\STACKER\SYSINFO.EXE

   COPY C:\CONFIG.SYS

   COPY C:\DOS\DBLSPACE.BIN

   COPY G:\STACKER.INI

   You do not need to rehide your Stacker Compression files; they are rehidden when you reboot your computer.

7. Edit the CONFIG.SYS file on the diskette in drive A so that only the following line remains:

   ```
   files=30
   ```

8. Try rebooting your computer with this diskette in drive A. Verify that it starts up with the A:\> prompt rather than the usual C:\> prompt. Verify that you can access the files on drive C.

9. Remove the diskette from drive A, write-protect it, and label it as a bootable Stacker diskette. Then, store the diskette in a safe place.

10. Restart your computer from your hard disk.

11

What do I do if I have installed Stacker and now my computer will not start?

If your system will not start up at all on drive C, the Stacker configuration files or DOS system files may be missing or corrupted. You can copy them back to drive C using your PC DOS setup diskette or a Stacker start-up diskette.

Note: *You should use a backup copy of your setup diskette for this procedure. If you have not already made one, do so now. See Chapter 2, "Making DOS Work," for information on copying diskettes. Creating a Stacker start-up diskette is covered in the preceding section.*

To Restore the Stacker configuration files, follow these steps:

1. Insert the backup copy of the setup diskette from your PC DOS installation diskettes into drive A and restart your computer.

2. Press **N** for No when queried if you want to install DOS.

3. At the PC DOS command prompt, type the following:

   C:\STACKER\CONFIG

   If your Stacker files are stored in a directory other than C:\STACKER, use that directory name.

4. Press **Enter**.

   If you have a Stacker start-up diskette, you can use it in place of the PC DOS setup diskette.

5. Agree to any changes that DOS or Stacker suggests.

6. When the PC DOS command prompt is displayed again, remove the diskette from drive A, and restart the computer again.

If the computer still does not restart from drive C, you may have to restore the DOS system files as well.

To restore the DOS system files, follow these steps:

1. Insert your setup diskette into drive A and restart your computer.

2. Press **N** for No when asked whether you want to install DOS.

3. At the PC DOS command prompt, type the following:

   C:\STACKER\STACKER

   This command lists your drive map. If your Stacker files are stored in a different directory, specify that directory.

4. Identify the drive letter of the uncompressed boot drive (in brackets at the end of the drive C line).

5. At the PC DOS command prompt, type the following:

   SYS *drive:*

   where *drive:* is the uncompressed drive letter.

6. Remove the setup diskette from drive A and restart your computer.

If your computer still will not start up from drive C, you might have a problem with your DOS version. Check the PC DOS 7.0 Command Reference for more information.

What should I do if my computer starts, but I cannot access compressed data?

When the computer appears to start up normally, but you cannot find your compressed data, it usually means that the Stacker drive was not mounted. To verify that the Stacker drives were not mounted, type the following at the PC DOS command prompt:

C:\STACKER\STACKER

If STACVOL files are not listed, they were not mounted.

To mount a Stacker drive temporarily, type the following at the PC DOS command prompt:

STACKER *drive:*

where *drive:* is the disk that contains the STACVOL file.

When you restart your computer, the specified drive will be **unmounted** again.

If you see a message that there are no available replaceable drives, you must edit the STACKER.INI file to add an RP command. On a new line, type **/RP=2**. If you already have an RP command, increase its value by at least one.

To mount a Stacker drive permanently, follow these steps:

1. Edit the STACKER.INI file to cause a converted drive to be mounted when you restart your system and add a drive-specification line. For example, on a new line, you would type the following:

   ### *drive:*\STACVOL.dsk sw

2. Restart your computer to mount the drive, along with any other drives specified in STACKER.INI.

How can I rebuild the Stacker configuration?

If you must rebuild the Stacker configuration, follow these steps:

1. At the PC DOS command prompt, change to the usual boot drive (usually drive C) and type the following:

   ### C:\STACKER\CONFIG

   CONFIG searches for STACVOL files and builds the entries needed to configure the basic system.

   Changes you may have made to the basic system will revert back to original settings, so you will have to make modifications again.

2. Restart your computer.

Why is my Stacker drive write-protected?

When an application exits improperly, a damaged file—such as a temporary swap file, a holding file, or a document—may be left behind. This damage is present whether or not Stacker is on your system. The next time you restart your computer, Stacker's AutoProtect notices the problem and tells you what to do. When CHECK /WP runs from your AUTOEXEC.BAT file, it automatically repairs the damage, removes the write protection, and restarts your computer.

11

If you are not sure whether the disk still is write-protected, run CHECK /F. If any problems remain, CHECK fixes them and removes write-protection for you.

What does this message mean?

```
Detected a Restart While Stacker Optimizer Was
Writing
```

The system was restarted while the Stacker Optimizer was in the `Writing New Directories...` stage of optimization. The program must finish what it started to put the STACVOL file in usable condition. Your data is safe, but you cannot access it until Stacker can mount the drive.

Do not restart your computer while the Stacker Optimizer is running. If you must interrupt it, press **F10** to exit safely.

To let Stacker Optimizer continue, follow these steps:

1. Determine the STACVOL file name (use the STACKER command, if necessary).

2. Insert the setup diskette and change to that drive (or change to the Stacker installation drive and directory), and type the following:

   SDEFRAG /ReSTORE=*drive:*\STACVOL.XXX

   where *drive:* is the uncompressed drive and *xxx* is the file extension of your STACVOL file (most likely DSK).

3. Let Stacker Optimizer continue working. When finished, it restarts your computer and mounts the Stacker drive.

What does this message mean?

```
Detected a Restart While Stacker Optimizer Was
Optimizing Files
```

The system was restarted while Stacker Optimizer was in the `Optimizing files...` stage of optimization. Stacker write-protected the Stacker drive to protect your data. You will have to let the Optimizer repair the Stacker drive. Then, restart to remove the write protection.

To complete Stacker Optimizer and remove the write protection, follow these steps:

1. At the PC DOS command prompt, type the following:

   SDEFRAG *drive:*

where *drive:* is the Stacker drive. The SDEFRAG command repairs the drive and restarts your computer.

2. Run CHECK /F. Then run Stacker Optimizer again.

What does this message mean?
```
Unable To Repair FATs, #139 (SDEFRAG)
```

If SDEFRAG is not able to repair the Stacker drive in the preceding situation, you see this message. It means that both copies of the File Allocation Table (FAT) have been corrupted. You will lose some data if you follow this procedure, but it is the only way to save the remaining data on your disk.

To repair the FAT and get rid of damaged files, follow these steps:

1. At the PC DOS command prompt, make the Stacker drive current and type the following:

CHECK/=A /F

Note: *Be careful when using the /=A parameter.*

2. When CHECK offers to repair the drive, let it.

3. When CHECK offers to delete files, answer **N**o.

4. Restart your computer and run CHECK /F again. Let it delete any files still reported as damaged. Then, use your most recent backup to restore missing files.

Troubleshooting Other Stacker Problems

This section explains how to deal with some problems that may occur occasionally while you are using Stacker.

Stacker Optimizer and 32K Clusters

If you use drives with 32K clusters, Stacker Optimizer may need more memory (more than the 600K needed in previous Stacker versions). If you do not have that much conventional memory available, run Stacker Optimizer with a special option. Using this option affects speed, but it enables you to run Stacker Optimizer using less memory.

11

To run Stacker Optimizer with less memory, follow these steps:

1. Exit Windows completely.

2. From the PC DOS command prompt, type the following:

SDEFRAG/BUFFER=*nnn*

where *nnn* is a value between 256 and 4096. By default, SDEFRAG normally runs at /buffer=4096.

The following examples show how much memory you can save with various values:

sdefrag /buffer =3072	21K memory saved
sdefrag /buffer =2048	42K memory saved
sdefrag /buffer =256	78.75K memory saved

Read, Write, and Media Errors While Optimizing

When you run the Stacker Optimizer, SDEFRAG reads, writes, and verifies every bit of data on your Stacker drive. In the process, it may come across disk surface errors, inconsistencies in the file, or directory structures on the disk. It cannot continue until these are fixed.

Depending on your system and the exact problem, you may see any of these message numbers: 109, 110, 112, 118, 120, or 170. All these numbers indicate that the Stacker Optimizer found an error on your disk while attempting to read, write, verify, or decompress a file. The problem may be in the file allocation table (FAT) or on the disk itself.

When you get one of these messages, it is a good idea to back up your data if you have not done so recently. If the message indicated a read error (109 or 120), however, you will not be able to back up until you correct the problem.

There are two steps to finding and fixing the problem. First, run a surface-scan utility on the uncompressed drive to deal with media problems. Then, run a read scan on the Stacker drive to deal with any resulting data problems.

To identify and correct the problem, follow these steps:

1. Repair the uncompressed drive using a utility such as Central Point's PC Tools DiskFix.

   Message 170 indicates a serious problem. First, run a tool such as Central Point's PC Tools DiskFix. If it finds a problem and offers to fix it, let it. If it does not find any problems, however, you must run Calibrate, which takes more time but is more thorough.

2. Run CHECK /F to find and repair data-structure problems on the Stacker drive.

3. When CHECK asks whether it should do a surface scan, let it.

If you prefer, you can use a disk-repair utility to perform a read scan of the Stacker drive. You will have to add a command to the STACKER.INI file first.

To scan the Stacker drive with another utility, follow these steps:

1. Use the PC DOS E Editor to add the /R command to the beginning of your STACKER.INI file.

2. Restart your computer. Then, run a disk-repair utility such as PC Tools' DiskFix on the Stacker drive.

3. Remove the /R switch (it is only for diagnostic use), and restart your computer.

4. Use Check Drive Integrity in the Stacker DOS toolbox and follow the instructions. Let CHECK delete any damaged files.

What do I do if I accidentally deleted my last Stacker drive?

If you choose to uncompress Stacker drives, after your last (or only) Stacker drive is uncompressed, you are prompted as to whether you want to remove the Stacker driver from your system. You should answer **No**.

If you answer **Yes**, you will need to re-create your DBLSPACE.BIN file. If you have a bootable Stacker diskette, you can just copy the DBLSPACE.BIN file from the diskette back into your \DOS directory, and the STACKER.COM and STACKER2.BIN files back into your \STACKER directory.

If you do not have a bootable Stacker diskette, follow these steps:

1. Change to the Stacker directory.

2. At the PC DOS command prompt, type the following:

   COPY /B STACLOAD.BIN + STACKER.COM DBLSPACE.BIN

3. Locate and copy the DBLSPACE.BIN file to the root directory of the boot drive (usually drive C).

4. Copy the STACKER2.BIN file from the Stacker directory to your root directory.

5. Reboot your system to reload the Stacker driver.

After rebooting, you can rerun Stacker to create new Stacker drives.

Index